IMAGES
of America

COLLEGE PARK

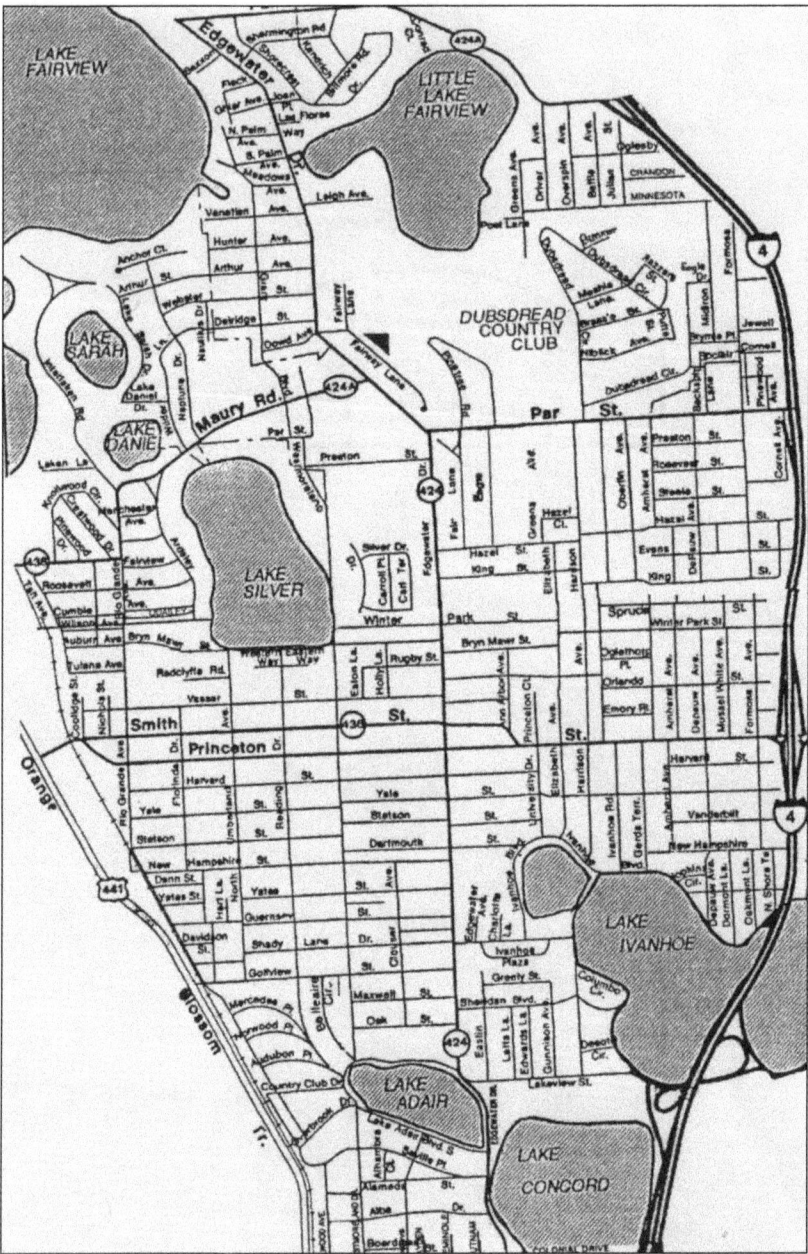

The modern-day College Park neighborhood encompasses the area between West Colonial Drive on the south, Fairbanks Avenue on the north, the Orange Blossom Trail on the west, and North Orange Avenue on the east. Edgewater Drive, College Park's main street, runs north and south through the center of the community. (Courtesy of College Park Neighborhood Association.)

ON THE COVER: In 1933, these seven College Park mothers celebrate their children's birthdays at 39 East Harvard Street, the home of Erna Hoskins, fourth from left with her son, Jimmy. Among the guests were Dorothy Lee, second from left with her daughter, Virginia; Sue Rives, third from left with Bettye Ann; and Elsie Griffin, sixth from the left with her daughter, Barbara. (Courtesy of Virginia Porter.)

IMAGES
of America

COLLEGE PARK

Tana Mosier Porter
for the College Park Neighborhood Association

ARCADIA
PUBLISHING

Published by Arcadia Publishing
Charleston, South Carolina

Library of Congress Control Number: 2014945562

For all general information, please contact Arcadia Publishing:
Telephone 843-853-2070
Fax 843-853-0044
E-mail sales@arcadiapublishing.com
For customer service and orders:
Toll-Free 1-888-313-2665

Visit us on the Internet at www.arcadiapublishing.com

To Fred and Grace Hagedorn for all you have done for College Park.

CONTENTS

ACKNOWLEDGMENTS

Grace Hagedorn inspired this work, and her 30 years of painstaking research inform every page. Any errors or misinterpretations are mine. Many others offered valuable assistance, among them Nick and Caryn Acompora, Ruth Armstrong, Janice Banks, Robert Barnes, Joshua Beaty, Judy Becker, Debra Booth, Debra Bremiller, Carrie Busbee, Richard Camnitz, Louis Campese, Phoebe Carpenter, William Castlen, Margaret Chapman, Marion Chavarie, Grace Chewning, Ellyn Coalter, College Park Baptist Church, *College Park Community Paper*, College Park Methodist Church, Deborah Cook, Dennis Cone, Carl Dann III, Wilma DiGilio, Carolyn Dixon, Edgewater High School, Michele Erickson, the estate of Beulah Roney Drake, the estate of Lois and Esther Burke, Laurel Everson, Marilyn Ferris, the *Florida Catholic*, Linda Flynn, Debbie Goetz, Steve Gunter, Stacye Hill, Mary Holmes, Doris Huckleberry, Bertie Hunt, Incarnation Catholic Church, Bill Jennings, Kelsey Construction Inc., the Kelsey family, Lake Silver School, Peter Lam, Larry Limmel, Valeria Lopez, Cynthia McInvale, Elizabeth Magee, Monarcha Marcet, Lana Mathews, Mills & Nebraska, Todd Mondok, William Morgan V, Edmond Moses Jr., Orlando Junior Academy, Betty Pallone, Bunny Parish, Carol Parker, Diane Patrick, Courtney Peacock, Virginia Porter, Barbara Powers, Luanne Preston, Princeton School, Bridget Pulsifer, Nancy Rodlun, Anne and Buddy Rogers, Andronidus Rollins, Jane Roney, St. Michael's Episcopal Church, Irma Scudder, Reva Shader, Jackie Sneed, Pat Spencer, Robert Stuart, Cynthia Swanson, Lynda Swenk, the Tap Room at Dubsdread, Bonnie Tew, Thelma Tice, Peggy Jo Van den Berg, and Julie Williams.

INTRODUCTION

In February 1925, David Cooper, S.H. Atha, and Harry Barr drove their Model T Fords to the foot of Dartmouth Street where it meets the shore of Lake Ivanhoe to break ground for a new development they named College Park. They platted 201 building lots on a 40-acre parcel of land that stretched from New Hampshire Street to Princeton Street and from Edgewater Drive past University Drive to Rose Terrace. This marked the first use of the name College Park, but not the first use of college names. Walter W. Rose had first named the streets for Ivy League colleges in his Rosemere development in 1921, and the Cooper-Atha-Barr Real Estate and Mortgage Company continued the college street names. In all, the company platted nine developments with variations on the College Park name and all with streets named for colleges.

Developers believed that clever names and impressive entrance gates would sell building lots, and perhaps they did. However, nearly 100 years before the area became College Park, people seeking land had lived there as squatters with no title or claim to the land. Many fled to safety during the Second Seminole War, which began in the area around 1835. They returned when the war was over in 1842 to find government surveyors at work, statehood pending, and legitimate claimants on the land.

To prepare for statehood, surveyors laid out all of Florida in a grid system of ranges of regular square townships based on the north-south meridian and an east-west baseline. The system originated with the Land Ordinance of 1785 when the United States sold land in the Western Territories to pay off debt from the Revolutionary War. It replaced the older method of surveying based on natural features such as trees, rocks, and creeks, which changed and sometimes disappeared, leading to contention over boundaries and ownership. The ranges, townships, and sections of townships provided a more reliable method of organizing saleable land. College Park encompasses six sections and parts of three others in Township 22 South, Range 29 East. Neighborhoods identified today as subdivisions originated as parts of Sections 10, 11, 12, 13, 14, 15, 22, 23, and 24.

The earliest-known College Park resident, Daniel K. Hall, served in Aaron Jernigan's company in the Second Seminole War and stayed in the College Park area after the war. Like most of the earliest inhabitants, he likely occupied the land as a squatter before he could legally own it. In 1868, Daniel and Sarah Hall paid the State of Florida 50¢ per acre for property in Sections 13 and 24, their first recorded land transaction. Their purchase lay between Lakes Ivanhoe and Formosa, where Hall at one time owned a small, water-powered gristmill in what became the town of Formosa. Another early College Park resident, William B. Hull, settled near Lake Fairview in 1856 in the area later known as Fairvilla, but moved on to Orlando less than four years later.

The first settlers cultivated the land on widely scattered farms, reportedly planting cotton. However, a bulletin published in 1884 by the US Department of the Interior contends that the soil in central Florida could not support cotton farming, and the only cotton successfully grown in Florida came from the counties adjacent to the Georgia border. Some Orange County landowners planted small amounts of cotton for extra cash, and one or two larger efforts around

Lake Apopka could be called plantations, but cotton never dominated the economy. The federal bulletin records that the cultivation of tropical fruit soon eclipsed that of cotton.

The Civil War slowed settlement, but when the war ended, newcomers to central Florida could take advantage of the Homestead Act of 1862, passed during the war to attract settlers to the western frontier and to promote railroad construction. For the first time, people could obtain free land—one quarter section or less, up to 160 acres. To gain clear title to the land, pioneers had to reside on their claim for five years, build a cabin, clear the land, and plant crops. Not all of the farmers who attempted to fulfill the terms of the Homestead Act found themselves able to cope with the isolation of frontier life and some returned home, forfeiting their claims. At least nine people proved their homestead claims in College Park; the number of claimants who failed is unknown. Successful College Park homesteaders included Benjamin F. Hull in 1875; Charles Roberson, John Ericsson, and James Patrick in 1878; William W. Barber and Samuel Russ in 1882; and David Y. Russell and William M. Taylor in 1883.

In a surprising nod to equality of the sexes, the Homestead Act granted single women homesteading rights equal to men if they were the heads of their own households. Annie E. Long acquired title in 1876 to two parcels she had homesteaded in Section 14 of College Park. Long sold most of her property, just south of modern-day East Princeton Street, almost immediately. Homesteaders and purchasers alike bought and sold real estate throughout the 1870s and 1880s, something of a precursor to the land boom of the 1920s.

An 1879 Orange County map shows communities at Formosa and Fairvilla, but no other evidence of settlement in College Park despite the many deed transactions recorded during the 1870s. Formosa developed near Princeton Street and North Orange Avenue in the 1870s. James Wilcox bought the land around 1880 and named the place Wilcox, but its name became Formosa in 1887. Bosse's Store housed the train station and the Formosa post office. Orange County records show a school at Formosa from 1877 until 1886. In Fairvilla, on the west side of College Park near Lake Fairview, the Fairview School opened in 1886 and held classes until 1927. A railroad station and post office south of Lake Fairview appeared on an 1890 Orange County map as the Livingston Station on John Livingston's property.

College Park's first boom began with the construction of the railroads, which brought reliable transportation to central Florida. The South Florida Railroad, completed to Formosa in 1880, ran down the east side of College Park, and in 1884, the Tavares, Orlando & Atlantic Railroad passed through Fairvilla on the west side of College Park. The railroads brought new residents and tourists, but more importantly, they enabled citrus growers to ship their fruit to northern markets more quickly and profitably, benefiting the regional economy.

The early maps show most of the land as prairies and swamps, but citrus groves, pineapple pineries, and grape vineyards, the tropical fruit of the Department of the Interior report, soon replaced the wilderness. In 1886, growers from the grape region of New York bought land in Section 14 and planted Niagara White grapes in a 200-acre vineyard they named Niagara Villa. The *Florida Agriculturalist* reported in 1892 that the vineyards of the Florida Niagara Vineyard Company bordered the railroad at Fairvilla and extended almost to the railroad at Formosa, northeast of Orlando. The Great Freeze in the winter of 1894 and 1895 killed the vines, but the lack of a central Florida market for wine and a shortage of ice for shipping the grapes north had already crippled the grape industry in College Park.

College Park remained barely populated grove land, distant from the developing city of Orlando in 1897, when T.J. Tucker deeded land to the Catholic Diocese of St. Augustine for the Catholic Cemetery on Edgewater Drive. An iron fence along Edgewater at what is now Langston Court protected the cemetery. In 1938, the diocese moved approximately 300 graves from the Old Catholic Cemetery to the new Woodlawn Cemetery in Ocoee, and sold the property between Guernsey Street and Shady Lane Drive to C.E. Langston, who platted the Oak Park subdivision the same year.

Some land owners platted subdivisions on their acreage in the hilly region around Lakes Ivanhoe, Concord, and Adair in anticipation of Orlando's expansion to the north, but their groves remained in production until that time came. Nathan F. Abbott entered his subdivision in 1884, John Childress and William Duncan in 1885, and Charles Joy platted his Joy's Addition in 1885, but little of the land sold as home sites until Orlando began annexing the area in 1904. The Concord Park Development Company platted Concord Park in 1909, and in 1911, Orlando's second annexation extended the northern city limits to Lakeview Street, north of Lake Concord. The large lots in the early subdivisions allowed other developers to purchase single lots and re-subdivide them into smaller, more saleable lots. Re-subdivision of Concord Park began in 1911, with five new plats entered by 1912.

More property around the lakes became potential home sites as C.W. Rowe platted his subdivision of Concord Park, and the Colonial Land Company platted Orange Park, both in 1914. Carl Dann's Development Company built in Concord Park in 1916, and in 1919, David Cooper and S.H. Atha purchased George Russell's amusement park and subdivided it as Ivanhoe Park. Walter W. Rose bought 26 acres in the Formosa area in 1920, which he began to plat in 1921. In 1925, groves still produced citrus fruit in the Ivanhoe section of Cooper-Atha-Barr's College Park, and the west side of Edgewater Drive remained mostly woods. By the end of the 1920s, realtors and developers had platted most of the land in what is now considered College Park.

The prospering real estate market of 1920 turned into the frantic Florida land boom, College Park's second boom, by 1925. Developers purchased tracts of land and platted subdivisions, putting in streets, sidewalks, and sometimes water, lights, and sewers in anticipation of quick sales to the northern buyers arriving by the hundreds. Some developers provided well-constructed houses, others put up cheap houses of stucco on lathe, and some built no houses at all, preferring to sell to builders or speculators. So-called "binder boys," independent salesmen wearing golf knickers, swept into Florida and bought building lots for 10 percent down. The binder, or receipt for the down payment, held the property for 30 days, but the binder boy had already sold the binder for more than he paid for it. Real estate men selling to each other accounted for much of the selling during the boom, but people excited about the whole idea of Florida and fearful of missing out on an opportunity to get rich bought whatever was available at any price. Property prices rose as binders sold and resold and the inflated land values affected the entire economy. The value of building permits increased every month.

The land boom faltered in 1926. Northern buyers, who had been assured that hurricanes presented no danger, hesitated after a disastrous hurricane hit Miami in 1926. For the first time, they took seriously the warnings about fraudulent land sales that were published in northern newspapers. Eventually buyers no longer came and the binder boys left town, leaving their notes unpaid. Too many individuals who bought houses or building lots for themselves defaulted on their mortgages on the overpriced land. The property reverted back to the developers, who went bankrupt trying to make the payments. The Cooper-Atha-Barr Company struggled to honor its commitment to repay mortgages if buyers defaulted. It sold at low prices to management companies and to builders who put up less expensive houses, but the company went bankrupt in 1929. Finally, even the banks failed.

During the 1920s, H. Carl Dann, Walter W. Rose, J. Carl Tegder, the Cooper-Atha-Barr Company, and other developers platted nearly 100 subdivisions and additions in College Park. With the exception of a few large show houses, little building took place during the Great Depression that followed in the 1930s. Some subdivisions remained partly vacant for years, with weeds growing up around the small stucco-covered houses built during the land boom. Large land management companies bought many abandoned houses after buyers defaulted on their loans and the banks failed. Some became rental properties. Beginning late in the 1930s, Wellborn Phillips bought more than 400 of the vacant properties, where he built more than 250 affordable houses for servicemen returning after World War II.

The postwar housing crisis, a sudden overwhelming demand for housing, became College Park's third and greatest boom. When building resumed at the start of World War II, military construction took precedence, and home-building materials went to the war effort. When the war ended, returning veterans needed houses. With employment high and with rationing during the

9

war, families had saved money, and government programs such as FHA and the GI Bill helped them acquire financing for houses that could not be built quickly enough. The vacant lots in College Park, left when the land boom collapsed, filled with houses as builders provided homes for young families.

Migration to Florida increased as military bases and the developing aerospace industry attracted new residents. Many settled in College Park, and the churches and schools expanded to accommodate new residents. New religious denominations established churches in College Park, and new schools opened. For the first time, businesses on Edgewater Drive multiplied, filling vacant properties with stores, offices, and gas stations. College Park flourished, and by the end of the 1950s, little land remained unused.

College Park developed essentially during two phenomenal housing booms. The earlier economic boost that came with the railroad spurred growth in the two small, semi-rural communities of Formosa and Fairvilla, but had little effect on the acres between them. From its beginnings in the 1850s until the land boom in the 1920s, groves, pineries, and vineyards took up most of that acreage. When the land boom ended, platted and improved subdivisions replaced the groves on most of the east side of Edgewater Drive and part of the west side. Many of the older houses in those blocks date to the first boom in the 1920s, when College Park first developed as a community. The remainder of the homes in the older blocks and many of the houses farther west of Edgewater Drive came during College Park's second boom, the postwar housing crisis. Infill construction eliminated vacant lots in the late 1940s and 1950s, and the children of the baby boom populated the schools, churches, and neighborhoods. In both boom eras, newcomers arrived as part of a wave of other new residents, brought together by common circumstances to become a community. In College Park, the values of small-town America developed with the community, and those values endure after 90 years of growth and change.

One

GROVES, PINERIES, AND VINEYARDS

Settlement of College Park began in the 1870s with the town of Wilcox (Formosa), near Lake Ivanhoe and the community of Fairview (Fairvilla), south of Lake Fairview. Between the two lay a large tract of sparsely settled citrus groves, pineapple pineries, and grape vineyards. The land came into private ownership during the 1870s and 1880s, with some homesteading quarter sections, but most purchasing property from the state for as little as 50¢ per acre. Few of the owners settled on their properties, and many never lived in Florida.

Both Formosa and Fairvilla boasted railroad stations, schools, and post offices at various times. In 1908, the Florida Sanitarium, now Florida Hospital, opened near Formosa, and in 1912 several Jewish families arrived in Fairvilla to establish dairy farms. Fairvilla, settled later and devoted to dairies and citrus groves, remained rural, while Formosa became a compact and organized town of more than 100 people by 1913, with the hospital and surrounding groves for support.

As the citrus industry recovered from the Great Freeze of 1894 and 1895, Orlando began to expand northward toward Lakes Ivanhoe, Adair, and Concord, where developers platted College Park's first additions in 1909. The city annexed the territory in 1911, followed by most of the remainder of College Park in 1923. The area became more residential after 1900, as pineapple growers near the lakes sold their pineries for subdivisions, and the large houses scattered among acres of citrus groves gave way to regular streets of smaller residences. North of the lakes, the citrus groves remained until the 1920s, when rampant development made the land too valuable for agriculture.

John and Minnie Ericsson homesteaded land near Formosa in 1875, and with James and Mary Harper, established a grove of 1,000 citrus trees. They built this house at 19 West Princeton Street, one of the two oldest in College Park, around 1882. A number of people owned the property after John Ericsson died in 1883. Charles Joy, who took possession when Ericsson's heirs defaulted on the mortgage, sold the grove to realtor John Sinclair. Sinclair offered the grove "overlooking beautiful Lake Ivanhoe" and "a nearly new two-story house" for sale in 1885 at an asking price of $16,000. In 1900, Charles Trevor failed to pay back taxes and Joseph and Martha Johnson acquired the property. They sold the grove to pay the mortgage in 1923, but the house remained in the family until 1948. (Courtesy of Dennis Cone.)

In 1882, John G. Sinclair bought land near the settlement of Formosa, where he built a large house he called La Esperanza. Beulah Roney, pictured on the horse, enjoys a visit to La Esperanza in 1914. One of College Park's two oldest houses, now at 226 Vanderbilt Street, it became the home of Sen. Walter W. Rose. (Courtesy of estate of Beulah Roney Drake.)

Few early landowners occupied their College Park properties. Some lived elsewhere in Orlando, while others, the original "snowbirds," only wintered in Florida and employed caretakers to manage their vineyards, groves, and pineries. Alex and Mamie Lashbrook lived at La Esperanza but probably did not own the grove when Beulah Roney, second from left, visited in 1914. (Courtesy of estate of Beulah Roney Drake.)

In 1888, Melvin Cone was living in Baltimore when he purchased land in the Formosa area. He claimed residence in Orange County when he bought additional land there in 1891. In 1911, Melvin and his wife, Mary Jessie, sold the property to their son Richard. The sale included the Cone homestead at 311 West Princeton Street, shown here in 1893. (Courtesy of Dennis Cone.)

History credits Nathan Abbott with naming Lake Ivanhoe for the eponymous hero of Sir Walter Scott's novel *Ivanhoe*. Abbott bought 40 acres on Lake Ivanhoe in 1879, where he built a large house. He also platted Abbott's subdivision in 1884. The Abbotts, New York City residents, probably only wintered on Lake Ivanhoe, shown here in a later photograph. (Courtesy of Grace Hagedorn.)

Elizabeth Avenue appears peaceful a century after Augusta Kollock bought property on Lake Ivanhoe from Marshall Porter in 1877 and named it Tranquila. Porter bought it from the state in 1876 for $1.25 per acre, and in 1882, Augusta sold her acreage when she married William Eppes. Walter Rose acquired it in 1923 and platted his Rose Terrace subdivision there in 1924. (Courtesy of William Morgan.)

Fishermen cast their nets in the run between Lakes Adair and Concord in this 1893 photograph. John Childress, who bought a grove near the lake in 1884, named it Lake Adair for his wife, the former Mary Adair Lyon. Childress, a judge in Nashville, Tennessee, and a snowbird, platted a subdivision near Lake Adair with William Duncan in 1885. (Courtesy of State Archives of Florida, Florida Memory.)

College Park's Lake Concord, shown here in the mid-1880s, provided recreation as well as fertile ground for tropical fruit. In 1909, H. Carl Dann's Concord Park Development Company platted Concord Park subdivision between Lakes Concord and Adair, the first planned development in what would later become College Park. (Courtesy of State Archives of Florida, Florida Memory.)

Early landowners, having found the soil and climate around College Park's lakes favorable for growing tropical fruits, planted the orange groves and pineapple pineries on Lakes Concord and Ivanhoe, shown here in 1905. George Russell's pinery on Lake Ivanhoe, one of the largest, included 12 acres covered by shade cloth. As Orlando's population expanded to the north, subdivisions and residences replaced the pineries, groves, and vineyards. (Author's collection.)

Shooting the Chute at Russell's Pavilion, Orlando, Fla.

Unable to compete with free-trade Cuban pineapples, George Russell closed his pinery by 1910. In its place, he built a park on Lake Ivanhoe with a dance hall and docks for swimming and boating. Originally Russell's Point or Pavilion, a contest renamed the popular park Joyland. In 1919, Russell sold the park to the Cooper-Atha-Barr Company, which platted the Ivanhoe Park subdivision on the site. (Courtesy of State Archives of Florida, Florida Memory.)

Formosa expanded in 1908 with the opening of the Florida Sanitarium on wooded property between Lakes Winyah and Estelle. The Seventh-day Adventist hospital, with 20 beds, two doctors, and a herd of dairy cows, offered a rest cure for tuberculosis and other diseases. Shown here about 1908, it appeared and operated more like a hotel than a hospital. (Courtesy of State Archives of Florida, Florida Memory.)

The Seventh-day Adventist Church organized a congregation in Orlando in 1890 and a church school in 1906. The school moved from downtown Orlando to the Florida Sanitarium property in 1908. It occupied several different buildings near the hospital before moving to its own building on Evans Street in 1925. This photograph of the first graduates was taken around 1914. (Courtesy of Orlando Junior Academy.)

Despite this photograph's label, "Princeton Street, 1893," the Cleveland Automobile Company only produced cars from 1904 to 1909. The rutted, sandy road running through a palmetto and pine forest might have been Princeton Street or any other Florida road up to the 1920s. Statewide road improvements eventually enabled tourists to drive to Florida in their own cars, leading to the Florida land boom in the 1920s. (Courtesy of Dennis Cone.)

The Lake Fairview Spouting Well became a local attraction around 1912, drawing sightseers to the Davis-McNeill farm, later owned by the Nydegger family and now part of the Interlaken subdivision. The high-water drainage well, drilled in 1910 to regulate the water level in Lake Fairview, took in air along with the water until the air pressure became greater than the weight of the water in the well. The air pressure in the well forced the water to spout more than 100 feet into the air at 20-minute intervals. The farm manager, R.D. Eunice, charged a fee for viewing the "geyser" from the farm. Due to the spouting's interference with the well's drainage function, Orange County had the well capped in the 1930s. (Courtesy of Jerry Porter.)

College Park's Jewish community gathers for a picnic on the Shader farm around 1920. The Wittenstein, Levine, and Levy families moved from Pittsburgh to Orlando in 1912, followed by the Shader and Meitin families in 1913. Originally from Russia, they established citrus groves and dairy farms in Fairvilla. Three generations of Wittensteins farmed between Lakes Silver and Fairview. (Courtesy of State Archives of Florida, Florida Memory.)

From left to right in the back row, sisters Esther Shader Wittenstein, Fannie Shader Meitin, and Sarah Shader Miller, photographed around 1916 with their children Ruth Meitin, Joseph Wittenstein, Ralph Meitin, and Lilli Ann Miller, came to Florida in 1913 with their parents, Rose and Israel Shader. Israel Shader and Jacob Meitin established a dairy farm in Fairvilla, west of Lake Fairview, that operated until 1949. (Courtesy of State Archives of Florida, Florida Memory.)

The Jewish community gathered at Moses Levy's orange grove for orthodox religious services until 1919, when the congregation Ohev Shalom built a synagogue in Orlando. Levy's grove served as a social center as well. In 1917, the entire Jewish community celebrated the first Jewish wedding in Orlando when Aaron Levy married Rose Gliebman under a chuppah in his father's grove. (Courtesy of State Archives of Florida, Florida Memory.)

Fairvilla
School
1952

Fairvilla School, on Silver Star Road near Lake Fairview, operated from 1918 to 1955. An earlier school in the same vicinity, called Fairview School, opened in 1886 and closed in 1927. Fairview School had 16 students enrolled in 1915. Morita Mason Clark, principal of Fairvilla School, poses outside the school building in 1952. (Courtesy of Lake Silver School.)

This 1914 Fries map of Orange County shows the area that became College Park between Fairvilla and Formosa, with the 1845 surveyors' section numbers clearly indicated. The range, township, and section numbers made possible the orderly sale of land in Florida, and they remain a part of every property's identification for deed and tax purposes. All of College Park lies in Township 22 South, Range 29 East. The 1914 map shows vacant land and a few scattered roads that suggest little progress in College Park when compared to the regular platted streets in Winter Park and Orlando. Modelo Park, south of Fairvilla along the railroad, never became a town. Originally a large, prosperous pineapple pinery with its own station on the Florida Central & Peninsula Railroad, it later became a switching yard on the Seaboard Airline Railroad. (Courtesy of Orange County Regional History Center.)

Lake Ivanhoe, shown here in the 1950s, made a rapid transition from pineapples to recreation to residential development. David Cooper and S. Howard Atha, who formed a real estate partnership in 1912, bought George Russell's amusement park in 1919 and platted a subdivision on the west side of Lake Ivanhoe. Building lots in Ivanhoe Park sold out on the first day. (Courtesy of Grace Hagedorn.)

Orlando extended its boundaries north to Lake View Drive in 1913, annexing barely populated groves and scattered houses, including this frame house at 838 Ellwood Avenue in the Orange Park subdivision. Lester and Edna West bought the house in 1934, moved it to the back of the lot, and built a new house in front of it in 1938. (Courtesy of Mary Holmes.)

Residences replaced groves as Orlando expanded northward into the tropical fruit–growing region around Lakes Ivanhoe, Concord, and Adair in the early part of the 20th century. In 1920, Joe and Bertie Martin bought this property at 830 Ellwood Avenue in the Orange Park subdivision near Lake Adair, but the house likely predated the subdivision, platted by the Colonial Land Company in 1914. (Courtesy of Bertie Hunt.)

Boulevard around Lake Ivanhoe.

Automobiles and advertising made Orlando a popular winter vacation destination in the prosperous years after World War I. Wealthy visitors still came for the season, but the 1910 Good Roads Movement and expanding automobile ownership brought middle-class tourists to Florida for the first time. Civic organizations, railroads, and bus lines all joined the effort to draw people to Florida, particularly Orlando. (Courtesy of Jerry Porter.)

Two

FLORIDA LAND BOOM

College Park developed during several periods of rapid economic growth. The first boom came with the railroads in 1880, bringing land speculators and commerce to Formosa and Fairvilla. An economic growth spurt followed the recovery of the citrus industry after the Great Freeze of 1894 and 1895, and Orlando expanded northward to Lakes Adair, Concord, and Ivanhoe by 1910. Beginning in 1920, the phenomenon known as the Florida land boom dwarfed every previous experience. When it ended less than a decade later, subdivisions had replaced the groves in most of what is now College Park.

Americans emerged from World War I euphoric and prosperous. Oranges and warm weather attracted people to Florida, and they drove south in their own automobiles. They came as tourists, but soon discovered cheap land and the profits that could be made from buying and selling real estate. Aggressive advertising created a frenzied real estate market, and land was sold and resold, sometimes several times in one day.

Many buyers never visited their properties, but others built houses and moved their families to College Park. Churches and schools followed the population, and businesses opened along Princeton Street and Edgewater Drive.

The boom collapsed when northern buyers stopped coming, scared off by a hurricane that hit Miami in 1926 and reports of fraudulent land sales. The banks failed when new owners defaulted on their loans. Vacant lots outnumbered the houses in some subdivisions, and others remained little more than streets and sidewalks. The collapse led Florida into the Great Depression ahead of the rest of the country.

Developers platted most of College Park during the Florida land boom of the 1920s, rushing to create new subdivisions with streets and scattered houses among the native pine trees, as shown in this 1926 photograph. Most subdivisions included paved and unpaved streets, water, sewers, and electricity. Deed restrictions often specified the size and cost of any house built on the property. (Author's collection.)

Orlando annexed territory around Lakes Concord, Adair, and Ivanhoe in 1909 and 1911, but many planned building lots remained unused until the 1920s, when the Florida land boom attracted crowds of tourists hoping to become residents. The property at 712 Seminole Avenue, annexed in 1911, sat vacant until 1923, when J. Peterson built a $3,000 house. Edna Webb lived here with her parents in 1925. (Courtesy of Mary Holmes.)

In 1917, Franklin Boardman, a wealthy Orlando merchant and real estate agent, bought property near Lake Concord. He built a house on the land in 1920 to house his family during the construction of another house, built in 1921, and platted Boardman's Addition in 1922. A founder and supporter of the College Park Baptist Church, Boardman lived at 800 Edgewater Drive until 1943. (Courtesy of College Park Baptist Church.)

Walter W. Rose came to Orlando in 1909 and entered the real estate business around 1913. In 1920, he bought property in the Formosa area and platted Rosemere in 1921. Rose, a state senator from 1933 to 1949, chose collegiate names for the streets but named his subdivisions for himself. (Courtesy of State Archives of Florida, Florida Memory.)

27

Walter Rose platted developments and sold building lots, but he never built houses. Rose sold property in his Rosemere subdivision in 1924, and the new owner, who probably built this house at 106 East Harvard Street, sold it the following year to W.S. Godley, who sold it to Mary Heisley in 1926. She kept the house as a rental until 1941, about the year this photograph was taken. (Courtesy of Bill Jennings.)

The 1882 Ericsson House, photographed around 1900, still stands at 19 West Princeton Street. Walter Rose bought the property in 1920 for his Rosemere Annex, platted in 1924. Joseph and Martha Johnson acquired it in 1902, and their daughter Mary Jessie Cone acquired it after a tax sale in 1929. She lived there until she sold it to her son Richard in 1948. (Courtesy of Dennis Cone.)

Eugene W. Kelsey Jr. started out as a building contractor in 1920 in College Park. Headquartered at 127 East Princeton Street, his family-run company built houses, churches, schools, hospitals, and military installations. In the 1930s, Kelsey Construction moved into a new corporate headquarters building. The company moved again in the 1950s to 306 East Princeton Street, after Interstate 4 construction eliminated its original location. (Courtesy of Kelsey Construction Inc.)

Kissam Builders and Supply Company began in 1922 as the Kissam Building Stone Company, producing and selling concrete and fireproof building materials on the northeast corner of Lake Ivanhoe. By 1925, as Kissam Builders' Supply Company, the firm produced Kissam's Tile, among other concrete products. (Courtesy of Mills & Nebraska.)

Trucks built to mix concrete en route to the job first made their appearance in the 1920s as concrete construction gained popularity. This Transit Mix Concrete Inc. truck, photographed on Mills Street around 1938, delivered concrete for several building supply companies located near Lake Ivanhoe and North Orange Avenue. (Courtesy of Mills & Nebraska.)

In 1924, Theodore and Carrie Tice bought property in Ivanhoe Terrace near Formosa. In this photograph they joined their children (from left to right) Emily, Jack, and Elsa in the yard outside their home, built a year or two before they bought it. The thriving town of Formosa ceased to exist after Orlando annexed the area in 1923. (Courtesy of Thelma Tice.)

John Chaffer built a playhouse for his grandchildren Jack, Emily, and Elsa in the yard at the Tice family home. This photograph of the children and their friends playing outside suggests the rural nature of Formosa in 1925, just after Orlando annexed the town. (Courtesy of Thelma Tice.)

Hanford Carl Dann, known as the most active real estate man in Orlando and an avid golfer, established a golfing community north of Par Street in 1923. He named the golf course Dubsdread because novice golfers, or "dubs," would dread playing on it. Dann's son, Carl Morris Dann, an amateur golf champion in the 1930s, learned to play at Dubsdread. (Courtesy of Carl Dann III.)

Four generations of the Dann family pose for a photograph in 1935. From left to right are Mary Dann, H. Carl Dann's mother; Hanford Carl Dann, College Park real estate developer and founder of the Dubsdread Golf Course; his son, Carl Dann Jr., five-time Florida state amateur champion golfer; and two-year-old Carl "Sandy" Dann III, representing the fourth generation. (Courtesy of Carl Dann III.)

In 1923, Orlando developer H. Carl Dann formed the Orlando Golfers' Association to build the Dubsdread golf course and country club on the northern edge of College Park. The first nine holes of the course Dann laid out with golf course designer Donald Ross opened in 1924, and the second nine were made available two years later. Dubsdread hosted amateur tournaments throughout the 1920s. (Courtesy of the Taproom at Dubsdread.)

Golf courses attracted homebuyers, and Carl Dann's Orlando Golfers Association sold many of its nearly 500 building lots in the Golfview and Dubsdread subdivisions before the golf course opened. Twins Graham and Gracia Barr grew up in the house their parents, Leal and Grace Barr, bought in 1924 at 3438 Fairway Lane, near the 12th green. (Courtesy of Nick and Caryn Acompora.)

In the booming 1920s, developers bought lots in existing subdivisions and carved them into smaller lots in new subdivisions. Brothers Charles and George Dudley subdivided A.J. Vaughn's 1912 replat of two lots of the 1909 Concord Park Addition, creating Dudley's subdivision in 1924. C.S. Hoag bought lot three in 1925 and built this house at 743 Edgewater Drive in 1927. (Courtesy of Julie Williams.)

Richard Cone bought lot six of Charles Joy's subdivision in 1914. He platted the west 200 feet of that property into building lots and entered it as the Oakdale subdivision in 1923. In 1924, he took out a permit to build a one-story frame house and a garage to cost $3,150. He built on lot one of his Oakdale subdivision in 1924, when Princeton Street was still a dirt road and Amherst Avenue, also dirt, was called Melvin Street. The Cone family owned the property until 1951 and the Cone children grew up in the house on the corner of Princeton Street and Amherst Avenue. In this photograph from about 1926, Richard's daughters, Helen and Mary Frances Cone, show off their kitten, their father's car, and their new house at 112 West Princeton Street. (Courtesy of Dennis Cone.)

John Burdick moved to Orlando from Virginia, expecting to prosper from the land boom. He bought and sold four properties between 1923 and 1927, including one in Rosemere Annex where he built the house at 103 West Princeton Street, shown here around 1930. Burdick sold that property to Hart Swalstead in late 1925 with the house unfinished. (Courtesy of Dennis Cone.)

Frank Eaton bought property in section 14 in 1906, before the land was platted and before Vassar Street existed. He took out a building permit in 1926 for a house, garage, and shed on the property at 823 Vassar Street. The rural setting of the house suggests little development in that part of College Park in 1926. (Courtesy of Grace Hagedorn.)

The Cooper-Atha-Barr Real Estate and Mortgage Company opened its College Park subdivision in February 1925 along Lake Ivanhoe at Dartmouth Avenue. Neither D.A. Cooper nor S.H. Atha appears in this photograph taken at the ground breaking, but pictured here from left to right are sales manager Bill Bingeman, unidentified, H.W. Barr, George Wettstein, B.H. Overpeck,

Charlie Allison, and R.W. Briscoe. This marked the first use of the name College Park, which the partners continued in eight additional subdivisions, all with streets named for colleges. (Courtesy of Orange County Regional History Center.)

The Cooper-Atha-Barr Company, developers of much of College Park, typically hired builders to put up one model house on each block of their new subdivisions. Those who bought the remaining lots built their houses in different architectural styles, including Mediterranean and Craftsman bungalows, as shown here. Only two houses occupied the block in this 1926 photograph, but the power pole indicates the availability of electricity. (Author's collection.)

This house at 823 Vassar Street looks more or less the same today as it did in this 1930s photograph, except for the car in the carport. The house first appeared in the city directory in 1929, and became part of the Eaton Park subdivision in 1964, when Albert Eaton platted six lots on Vassar Street, Eaton Lane, and Holly Street. (Courtesy of Grace Hagedorn.)

John Carl Tegder, born in Kansas, moved to Orlando in 1923 and went into the real estate business. He became known for his slogan, "Let's Talk It Over." In 1925, he opened his first subdivision, "Palm Terrace, the Beautiful," in College Park. Until his death in 1969, Tegder lived in a house he built on Bryn Mawr Street in Palm Terrace. (Courtesy of Julie Williams.)

Developer J. Carl Tegder's youngest daughter, Betty, posed happily on the little black pony an itinerant photographer led through the streets of College Park in 1924. Children flocked to the pony, and College Park parents could be counted on to buy photographs of their children. (Courtesy of Julie Williams.)

Carl Tegder's older daughters Jean and Ann shared a photograph with the pony that day in 1924. The photographer found the children on the well-landscaped grounds of the elegant rooming house on Colonial Drive where the Tegder family lived when they first arrived in Orlando the previous year. (Courtesy of Julie Williams.)

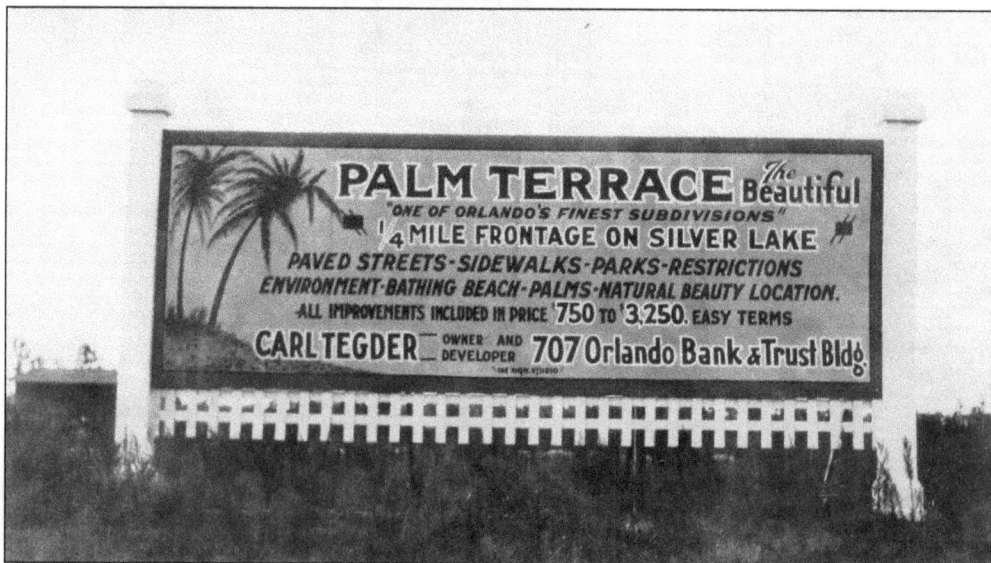

J. Carl Tegder platted his Palm Terrace subdivision on the northwest side of College Park in 1925. His advertising sign promised improvements included in the price, but the price determined the extent of the improvements. The restrictions indicated on the sign dictated the quality of the house to be built and the race of the occupants. (Courtesy of Julie Williams.)

Land boom developers believed that imposing entrance gates assured the success of any subdivision, so College Park developer Carl Tegder built the entrance to his 1925 Palm Terrace subdivision before he built the houses. He priced the 127 building lots according to whether they included paved streets or frontage on Lake Silver. Tegder supplied palm trees, 50¢ each, for landscaping. (Courtesy of Julie Williams.)

Ovil Eugene Inabnit bought a building lot in 1925, shortly after H. Carl Dann's Southern Development Company platted the Adair Park subdivision near Lake Concord in College Park. Inabnit, shown here with his wife, Lilly, and his children Elva, Sam Kinlaw, Nelva, Naomi, Winford Hester, and Merl Inabnit, built this unusual two-story house on Edwards Lane in 1925, using locally produced concrete blocks. (Courtesy of Marion Chavarie.)

O. Eugene Inabnit, who built the house at 1203 Edwards Lane in 1925, worked as a boilermaker for the Cain-O'Berry Boiler Company in Orlando and tended the boilers at the Angebilt Hotel. Two daughters missing from the earlier photograph, Daisy and Evelyn, joined in this 1950s Inabnit family portrait. (Courtesy of Marion Chavarie.)

Artist and builder Samuel Stoltz joined H. Carl Dann's Southern Development Company in 1926, designing houses in Adair Park, Dann's new development near Lakes Adair and Ivanhoe. Stoltz's work featured textured stucco walls, broken tile terraces, pecky cypress, unique stone fireplaces, and plaster and stucco relief birds. The flamingo shown here adorns the fireplace at 610 Greely Street. (Courtesy of Grace Hagedorn.)

Developer Walter Rose named Princeton Street in 1921. Originally known as Formosa Street, Princeton remained a barely developed dirt road in 1925 when Agnes Morgan and Arthur Newell were married in the living room of the house they had built at 1 East Princeton Street. Both worked as bank tellers, and Arthur Newell became Orange County clerk of courts. Their daughter Lois, born in 1926, grew up in that house in the Hillcrest Heights subdivision. She remembered hearing her mother speak of the large oak trees that once grew in the middle of Princeton Street, forcing cars to drive around them. After too many accidents when people failed to negotiate the curves, road workers cut the trees, allowing Princeton Street to be straightened and paved with brick. (Courtesy of William Morgan.)

Lois Newell plays with her doll on the front steps of her home at 1 East Princeton Street in 1932. Her parents, Arthur and Agnes (Morgan) Newell, sent for the house plans after they saw them in a magazine. The distinctive brick banisters set it apart from other houses built in College Park in the 1920s. (Courtesy of William Morgan.)

Arthur French bought this lot at 821 West Dartmouth Street in 1927. He sold it in 1932, still in debt for sewerage and paving. The Ohio resident probably never moved to College Park, but he kept his property longer than many who bought during the land boom. Mary Durr built on the lot in 1941. (Author's collection.)

By the mid-1920s, the Seventh-day Adventist church school felt the effects of the great Florida land boom in its overcrowded classrooms at the Florida Sanitarium property on North Orange Avenue. In 1924, Victor and Elizabeth Purvis donated four building lots on East Evans Street in College Park, where the school built a new $8,000 building. More than 100 students and three teachers made the move to the new campus, where the first classes met in the unfinished building in 1926. The school completed that building and several more, adding classes and programs and purchasing additional property in 1940 as attendance grew. Today, the church school continues its mission as the Orlando Junior Academy, enrolling students from preschool through ninth grade. (Courtesy of Orlando Junior Academy.)

Orange County opened several new schools in the 1920s as the school-age population outgrew the school buildings during the Florida land boom. After 1925, children living in the new subdivisions of College Park attended Concord Park Elementary School, at the southeast corner of Colonial Drive and the Orange Blossom Trail. (Courtesy of Bertie Hunt.)

Rufus Cranford sold 10 acres of land on Princeton Street to the trustees of the Orlando Special Tax School District No. 1 in 1925. He moved the house, shown here, to clear the site for the new Princeton Elementary School. The acreage originally belonged to Melvin and Mary Jessie Cone, who bought it in 1888 and lived there until 1905. (Courtesy of Grace Hagedorn.)

During the 1920s, newly platted, boom-time subdivisions north of Lake Ivanhoe brought more and more families to College Park. By 1926, the school-age population warranted an elementary school. Architect Howard Reynolds designed the tan stucco Princeton Elementary School, which opened at 311 West Princeton Street in January 1927 with Principal Evelyn Sharp and six teachers. (Courtesy of Princeton School.)

Community activities often revolve around neighborhood schools, and College Park residents quickly made Princeton Elementary the focus of their gatherings. The Princeton Singing Mothers, shown here during the 1929–1930 school year, undoubtedly doubled as a social organization and a fundraising committee. Money raised by such groups helped pay for trees and shrubs for new schools in need of landscaping. (Courtesy of Princeton School.)

College Park resident Ormund Powers poses in the back row in this 1929 photograph of Memorial Junior High students. Concord Park and Princeton Schools opened in the 1920s for elementary age children, but until the 1950s, all College Park junior and senior high school students attended Memorial Junior High and Orlando High School in downtown Orlando. (Courtesy of Barbara Powers.)

As Orlando's population spread north into College Park, the Orlando Fire Department built the city's third fire station to provide protection for the new subdivisions. Station Three opened in 1926 on Orlando Avenue near Dade Avenue, north of the intersection of Orange Avenue and Princeton Street. The two-story, redbrick fire station closed in 1973 after serving College Park for nearly half a century. (Courtesy of Dick Camnitz.)

Calvary Presbyterian Church, organized in 1924, purchased property at West Colonial and Edgewater Drives and built the church shown here in 1925. The congregation worshipped there until 1963, when they moved to Lee Road and sold the property at 709 Edgewater Drive to the First Church of Religious Science. In 2004, Calvary merged with John Knox Presbyterian, established in 1949, to become College Park Presbyterian Church. (Courtesy of Betty Pallone.)

The many families moving into College Park in the 1920s created a need for religious institutions in the community. In 1928, the First Baptist Church of Orlando helped to establish the College Park Baptist Church and contributed to the purchase of property on Edgewater Drive at Yale Street, where the congregation completed its first church building that same year. (Courtesy of College Park Baptist Church.)

College Park Baptist Church, organized in 1928, grew quickly to 73 members by 1930. F.N. Boardman donated property for a second building adjacent to the original church on Edgewater Drive. At the 1935 dedication of Boardman Hall, Franklin Boardman stands third from left, with Wilhelmina Boardman seated in front of him. Grandma Shockley and Grandma Yates sit at the right. (Courtesy of College Park Baptist Church.)

Ebbie Slayton Harrison bought the property at the intersection of Edgewater Drive and Smith Street in 1926, and her brother-in-law John Harrison took out a building permit for a two-story structure, to cost $11,000, and a $600 garage. They opened a grocery store in the building in 1930, which they continued to operate until 1950, renting the building after they defaulted on their mortgage in 1932. (Courtesy of Grace Hagedorn.)

Orlando Chamber of Commerce members and guests assembled for this photograph at Lake Eola in downtown Orlando following a March 1933 meeting. College Park developers J. Carl Tegder and Sen. Walter W. Rose joined the crowd in front of the sweet pea wall. (Courtesy of Julie Williams.)

The land boom collapsed in the late 1920s, leaving vacant lots and houses scattered throughout College Park. The Cooper-Atha-Barr Company built this $5,000 house at 733 Stetson Street in 1926 and sold it in 1930, but the house, shown here in 1951, stood vacant for more than a decade. The Lowndes Lippitt family lived in the house in the early 1950s. (Courtesy of Debra Bremiller.)

This photograph of the newly built house at 951 West Stetson Street shows the brick street, sidewalks, and electrical poles against a backdrop of vacant land and pine trees. The Cooper-Atha-Barr Company sold the lot in 1927, and the new owner built the house for $4,500 the same year. A year later the Prudential Insurance Company acquired the property, suggesting a foreclosure. (Courtesy of Phoebe Carpenter.)

Housing construction in the $5,000 or less range declined in the late 1920s, while the demand for larger, showy homes continued. This elegant house at 803 Lake Adair cost $26,000 to build in 1925. Brothers-in-law William Arthur and Charles Cavenaugh built a $12,000 house on Lake Concord at 1027 Edgewater Drive in 1925, and Grace Phillips Johnson's Mediterranean mansion at 1005 Edgewater cost $27,500 in 1928. (Courtesy of Grace Hagedorn.)

The subdivisions around Lake Adair tended to attract buyers who built larger and more elaborate houses than the rapidly spreading new subdivisions north of Lake Ivanhoe. The Gentile Brothers platted Edgewater Heights in 1924, and the lot at 926 Alameda Street sold several times before the Higginbothams took out a building permit in 1926. The house and garage they built cost nearly $10,000. (Courtesy of Grace Hagedorn.)

Raymond C. Stevens designed and built this Mediterranean Revival house at 1000 Cordova Drive in the Edgewater Heights subdivision in 1928. A real estate promoter in the 1920s described the area as "a combination of lakes, rolling high land, fine homes, broad streets, avenues of splendid trees, orange groves, a Country Club at the side door and a place close to the heart of town." (Courtesy of Grace Hagedorn.)

Pine trees and vacant lots separated the new houses on Princeton Street in 1930. With the land boom over, property no longer sold and the Cooper-Atha-Barr Company, which built the 801 West Princeton Street house in 1925, went bankrupt trying to cover mortgage payments on all their properties. Vacant for a time, then a rental for more than a decade, the house finally became owner-occupied in 1937. (Courtesy of Jane Roney.)

In 1933, when Barbara Ann Griffin celebrated her second birthday in the backyard of her home at 919 West Princeton Street, both her family and the family in the house next door rented their homes. After the land boom collapsed around 1926, real estate investment companies bought unsold houses or those in foreclosure, turning them into rental properties. (Courtesy of Barbara Powers.)

G.M. Sherman platted Shore Crest in 1925 and sold a building lot to Charles and Ida Flower the same year. The Flowers took out a building permit in 1926 for a single-story house to cost $5,000. They lived in the Mission Revival house at 1630 Oakmont Lane until 1928, when they sold to Firbmoco Corporation. The house remained vacant in 1930. (Courtesy of Grace Hagedorn.)

The Cooper-Atha-Barr Company probably built this house at 600 Dartmouth Street in the Ivanhoe Section of College Park. W.E. Martin bought the property from the developers in 1926, and immediately took out a permit to build a one-story addition. The Great Depression caught up with Martin, and Grace Bethea paid the back taxes and bought the house in 1932. (Courtesy of estate of Lois and Esther Burke.)

The Great Depression caught buyers and investors without funds, forcing H. Carl Dann (right) to reclaim properties, including Dubsdread. In 1931, he gave the golf course as a wedding present to his son Carl Morris Dann (left), five-time Florida amateur golf champion. Sandy Dann, the third golfer in this 1935 photograph, and his sister Joan became third-generation owners of Dubsdread. (Courtesy of Carl Dann III.)

Dubsdread Golf Course and Country Club became very popular during the late 1920s, before the Depression of the 1930s brought hard times and fewer golfers. In 1934, a fire destroyed the Mediterranean Revival clubhouse, shown here around 1930. Dann promised to rebuild quickly. His friend, architect and artist Sam Stoltz, designed a new clubhouse with his trademark stone fireplace and bird frescoes. (Courtesy of the Taproom at Dubsdread.)

56

Sam Stoltz designed and built a new clubhouse after the 1934 fire at Dubsdread as well as a house for the Dann family. Across Par Street, on Greens Avenue, the new home was constructed on the site of an older house, seen here under the pine trees around 1930. The new house featured the coquina stone fireplaces and bird frescoes that became Stoltz trademarks. (Courtesy of Carl Dann III)

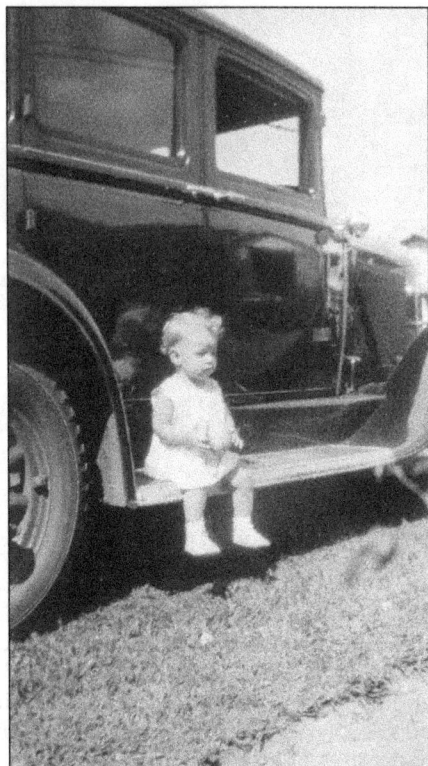

Pictured here in October 1932, Barbara Ann Griffin rests on the running board of the family car. The automobile contributed to the Florida land boom, and cars became an even greater necessity as developers platted new subdivisions distant from city centers. College Park boasted little industry and few businesses or stores in 1932, forcing residents to drive to Orlando for work or shopping. (Courtesy of Barbara Powers.)

In 1935, Princeton School first graders sit for their class photograph outside the school. Their teacher, Dicia George, stands behind them in the doorway. The large group of more than 30 students represented the significant expansion of College Park during the late 1920s and into the 1930s, despite the Great Depression. (Courtesy of Princeton School.)

Princeton Elementary School Parent Teachers Association officers and committee chairwomen, pictured here, gathered at the school in 1935. During the Depression, the Princeton School became an important community resource, helping students and their families with medical bills and other expenses, including eyeglasses for children whose poor vision jeopardized their education. (Courtesy of Princeton School.)

The Princeton Elementary School Parent Teachers Association 1935–1936 executive board assembled in front of the school for this photograph. Mrs. Compton, school principal, is on the right in the front row. As one of its projects in 1937, the PTA had the oak trees at the front of the school moved to the side yard, to be replaced with palm trees. (Courtesy of Princeton School.)

Princeton Elementary School principal Ruth Compton, on the left in the middle row, joined the sixth grade for their class photograph on the school lawn in 1937. Sixth grade teacher Marguerite Thomas appears on the right in the middle row. The students left College Park the following year to begin classes at Memorial Junior High School in downtown Orlando. (Courtesy of Princeton School.)

Princeton Elementary School graduate Col. Joseph Kittinger continued his education at Bolles Military School and the University of Florida. As a test pilot in the US Air Force, he contributed to aerospace medical research with a record jump from a balloon more than 19 miles high. Shot down flying combat missions in Vietnam, Colonel Kittinger spent 11 months as a prisoner of war in Hanoi. (Courtesy of Princeton School.)

Mothers and youngsters in their Sunday best line Edgewater Drive in 1934 to watch a children's parade. Barbara Ann Griffin, the little girl wearing the white hat on the tricycle, remembers the parade and bending down to look at the float passing by, but she does not remember the occasion for the festivities. (Courtesy of Barbara Powers.)

Young couples from Cherokee Junior High School demonstrate the dance moves they learned at the Pounds Dance Studio in College Park. Around 1935, Ruth Pounds began teaching ballroom dancing and etiquette to generations of teenagers in her home on Clifford Drive near Spring Lake. Classes concluded each year with a formal tea dance at the Country Club of Orlando. (Courtesy of Peggy Jo Van den Berg.)

Erna Achenbach emigrated from Germany in 1924 and followed the land boom to Florida in 1926. She started a kindergarten on Gerda Terrace in 1931, moved to 2312 Oberlin Avenue in 1933, and then to Emory Place in 1935. In 1939, her College Park Kindergarten met at 241 West Princeton Street where children, from kindergarten through the third grade, presented their annual Christmas program. (Courtesy of Irma Scudder.)

The Southerland family opened a filling station at 1807 Edgewater Drive in 1935, and the Southerland's Place bar in 1936. The number of businesses on Edgewater Drive declined going into the Great Depression, but the end of Prohibition in 1933 brought liquor stores and roadhouses. Southerland's Place, shown here in the 1950s, became Gabriel's Subs after Paul Gabriel bought the property in 1981. (Courtesy of Barnes Draperies.)

John Southerland poses outside Southerland's Place, the bar his sister Ina opened at 1807 Edgewater Drive in the 1930s. Dora Southerland joined her daughter in the business, which included a gas station, after the death of her husband, Rutherford Hayes Southerland, in 1947. A younger daughter, Elizabeth, married Lincoln Barnes in 1934. (Courtesy of Barnes Draperies.)

College Park's water tower rises above the trees behind Kathleen Keating and Gwen Derrick as they play with their cats on Princeton Street in this photograph taken around 1950. The 78-foot-high water tower on Rugby Street assured water pressure for College Park from 1938 until late 1991, when the Orlando Utilities Commission removed it. Improved city water mains rendered the light blue tower obsolete. (Courtesy of Doris Huckleberry.)

Marion sits with her dogs on the running board of a milk delivery truck in 1939. The Shader family in Fairvilla remained in the dairy business until 1949, but in 1939 they no longer delivered milk to customers in trucks like this one, having sold their milk route to Datson Dairy in 1918. (Courtesy of Bertie Hunt.)

Housing construction slowed during the Depression, but in the late 1930s, stately mansions appeared around the lakes in southern College Park. Architect James Gamble Rogers designed a $100,000 house for R.G. Coffey on Lake Ivanhoe in 1937, a $50,000 Georgian Colonial for R.D. Keene on Lake Adair in 1938, and in 1939, the palatial $26,000 Dr. McEwan home on Lake Concord, shown here. (Courtesy of Grace Hagedorn.)

Kiehl and Stevens built this frame and concrete-block house at 1131 Country Club Drive for Edward Jackson at a cost of $10,000 in 1938. Notable construction in 1939 included a house for George Carter at 550 Ivanhoe Plaza costing $15,000, and a $13,000 house for S. Evans at 809 Adair Boulevard North. (Courtesy of Anne and Buddy Rogers.)

D.J. Brass built this streamlined house at 610 Rugby Street for $3,000 in 1939. It first appeared in the city directory in 1940, one of only six houses on the block of Rugby Street between Ann Arbor Avenue and Edgewater Drive. William and Karolina Beese bought it in 1943 and lived there with their daughter's family for two years. (Courtesy of Grace Chewning.)

Wren's Red & White grocery store opened at Princeton Street and Edgewater Drive in 1939. The number of businesses on Edgewater Drive declined between 1930 and 1935, but then nearly doubled from 1935 to 1940, as depression gave way to war economy. College Park's population grew despite the Great Depression, and many new businesses like Ruby Wren Cole's grocery catered to the new residents' needs. (Courtesy of Bunny Parish.)

Betty Tegder, daughter of College Park developer J. Carl Tegder, pauses for photographs with her attendants at the Tegder family home at 743 Edgewater Drive before her marriage to C. Champ Williams on March 11, 1939, at the First Presbyterian Church in Orlando. The bridal party included friends from several prominent College Park families. From left to right are (first row) junior bridesmaid Marnay Meredith, Betty Tegder, and Betty's niece and flower girl Jo Ann McElroy; (second row) Elinor Voorhis, Betty Skelly, maid of honor Sara Sheeley, Betty Guernsey, Catherine Murphy, the bride's sister and matron of honor Ann McElroy, and Harriet Rose. (Courtesy of Julie Williams.)

Three

POSTWAR HOUSING CRISIS

World War II and the prosperous years that followed transformed College Park from a quiet village to a bustling town. The community prospered even before the war began when military personnel came to train at the nearby Orlando Army Air Base, often bringing their families with them. Housing construction essentially stopped during the war, as all building materials went to the war effort, but after 1946, when the government lifted wartime restrictions, home building took off dramatically. Building permits in Orlando in 1946 totaled more than $5.6 million, the highest in 20 years. In the late 1940s, apartment buildings went up around Lakes Ivanhoe and Concord, and between 1946 and 1955, small, inexpensive tract houses filled every vacant lot. College Park's population grew steadily after 1946, necessitating an additional elementary school, a junior high school, and two new high schools during the 1950s. Three new churches started in the 1940s and one in the 1950s. In 1948, residents asked for property to be set aside for a public park bounded by Dartmouth and New Hampshire Streets and Westmoreland and Edgewater Drives.

Edgewater Drive developed as a significant business district during the postwar years. About a dozen businesses operated on Edgewater Drive in 1940. Business development changed little by 1945, but grew by 1949 to more than 50 stores and offices. By 1955, the number of business places on Edgewater had more than doubled the 1949 total. In 1952 alone, a bank, post office, and the new high school opened on Edgewater Drive.

Dressed in his sailor suit, Myron Holmes plays with Kathleen Keating and an unidentified child in jodhpurs on Princeton Street in this 1940s photograph. The white building in the background on the right housed Wren's grocery store. The open space and many palm trees characterized College Park before the dramatic growth following World War II. (Courtesy of Doris Huckleberry.)

Princeton Elementary School celebrated May Day 1940 with a traditional May festival. About 300 students performed as fairies and elves in the pageant and danced around a maypole wound with colorful ribbons. More than 600 parents and friends gathered on the Princeton School lawn to see Jo Ann Cloud crowned Queen of May. Children from each grade served as attendants, trainbearers, and trumpeters. (Courtesy of Princeton School.)

Parents gathered on the lawn in front of Princeton Elementary School in 1941 to watch their children perform in the annual May Day Festival. During the 1940s and 1950s, many schools celebrated the first day of May with pageants, May queens and courts, dancing, music, and maypoles. (Courtesy of Princeton School.)

Outstanding Princeton Elementary School alumnus Capt. John Watts Young completed the sixth grade in 1942. Following his graduation from Orlando High School and the Georgia Institute of Technology, he became an officer in the US Navy and a test pilot. As an astronaut, John Young made six space flights in the Gemini, Apollo, and Space Shuttle programs and visited the moon twice. (Courtesy of Princeton School.)

Princeton Elementary School, shown here during the 1945–1946 school year, continued its role as the center of the College Park community 20 years after its opening in 1927. Orlando's growth in the 1940s and the arrival of the children of the baby boom generation required the addition of classroom wings behind the original building. (Courtesy of Princeton School.)

Princeton Elementary School's PTA continued to provide assistance to the school as College Park's population grew quickly after World War II. In this photograph, members of the 1946 PTA board pose on the steps of the school with the principal, Ruth Compton, in the front row. (Courtesy of Princeton School.)

Built in 1926, the block housing Harrison's Grocery Store stood alone on Edgewater Drive at the southwest corner of Smith Street in 1943, when Ray Lott stopped with his bicycle in the grassy lot across the street. Businesses filled the vacancies along Edgewater Drive in the years following World War II, when College Park experienced its second dramatic growth period, and the vacant lot at the southeast corner of Edgewater Drive and Smith Street soon became a construction site. George Fekany took out a building permit in 1946 for a store building on lots 14, 15, 16, and 17 of the College Park Golf Course Section G. The new store would cost an estimated $35,000. By 1948, Albert's Drug Store and the College Park Cleaners, as well as a number of smaller shops, had opened in the completed building. (Courtesy of Lana Mathews.)

Ebbie Slayton Harrison pats King Pen, the horse belonging to her son Slayton Harrison, at 726 West Stetson Street in 1943. Samuel and Ebbie Harrison and her brother Polk Slayton owned a grocery store at 2216 Edgewater Drive from about 1928 until 1950. Harrison also owned a service station at 2122 Edgewater Drive. (Courtesy of Lana Mathews.)

From left to right, Harrison's Grocery employees Lawrence Sateriano, Samuel Harrison, Charles Sage, and Bob Murdock stand in front of the store at 2220 Edgewater Drive in 1943. During World War II, service flags, like the star in the store window behind the men, hung in windows throughout the nation to show that a family member served in the military. (Courtesy of Lana Mathews.)

Military uniforms became a common sight in College Park during World War II. Ellis Fleming received his draft notice in 1944 when his younger son was eight months old. Shown here on leave at his home at 18 East Yale Street in 1944, he fought in the Battle of the Bulge and returned home when the war ended. (Courtesy of Bonnie Tew.)

World War II brought new residents to College Park, and with the expanding population came more religious diversity. The College Park Methodist congregation first met in the fall of 1943 in the Red Cross Center at 2216 Edgewater Drive. The congregation increased quickly from the original 19 adults and children to the 57 charter members shown here in January 1944. (Courtesy of College Park Methodist Church.)

The College Park Methodist Church broke ground for its first building in October 1944, on land the First Methodist Church of Orlando donated at the corner of Edgewater Drive and Princeton Street. The congregation helped finance the construction with "Block Sundays." Even the children saved their dimes to buy concrete blocks at 30¢ each. (Courtesy of College Park Methodist Church.)

The College Park Methodist Church held the first service in its new multi-purpose building on Christmas Eve 1944. This photograph shows the new education building, used for both Sunday school classes and worship services, opening on Princeton Street, with the College Park Texaco filling station at 2010 Edgewater Drive visible in the background. (Courtesy of College Park Methodist Church.)

74

The structure and the sailor in uniform suggest an early 1945 date for this worship service in the College Park Methodist Church education building. The congregation contributed enough money to complete its first building without borrowing, allowing them to begin raising money to build a sanctuary building two years later. (Courtesy of College Park Methodist Church.)

Operating with the same slogan, "Finish the Job—Keep out of Debt," the 277 members of the College Park Methodist congregation raised the money to build the redbrick church that today serves as the chapel. The new sanctuary, shown here during its construction in 1946, opened in 1947. (Courtesy of College Park Methodist Church.)

The College Park Methodist Church completed its new sanctuary in September 1947, adjacent to the original education building. Church membership increased as College Park's population grew, and the congregation paid for the entire construction of the church, shown here in 1959. (Courtesy of College Park Methodist Church.)

This 1959 photograph of the third grade class in the College Park Methodist Church school illustrates the effect of the population growth in the years immediately after World War II. These children, probably born about 1950, at the mid-point of the postwar baby boom, filled nearly every chair in the Sunday school room. (Courtesy of College Park Methodist Church.)

Ellis and Claudine Fleming bought this bungalow at 18 East Yale Street for $4,500 in 1941, with a mortgage payment of $39 a month. Rex-McGill Investment Company built the house, one of four the firm put up as speculation. The Flemings lived there until 1978 and raised two sons in the house. In this 1947 family photograph, Roger was about eight years old and Gary was four. (Courtesy of Bonnie Tew.)

Builder W.I. Cossin acquired this property at 526 Rugby Street after the previous owner, who had bought it from Cooper-Atha-Barr in 1927 and never built on it, defaulted on the mortgage. Cossin built a $6,000 concrete-block house in 1945, which he sold in 1946. Charles and Lucille McEwen bought it in 1947, and it remains in the family. (Courtesy of Debra Booth.)

Cabinetmaker Richard Summers built this $6,000 concrete-block house at 1115 West Smith Street on property he bought from J. Carl Tegder in 1945. Before World War II, builders generally employed frame construction, or stucco over wire lathe and frame. After the war, more durable concrete blocks became the most popular building material. Summers lived in the house until 1983. (Courtesy of Thelma Tice.)

After World War II, veterans coming home and newcomers seeking the warmth and sunshine they remembered from their training at Orlando's military bases all searched for housing where no vacancies existed. Builder Wellborn Phillips erected 10 houses on Shady Lane Drive in 1945, and individuals filled vacant College Park lots with houses like this one under construction at 1115 West Smith Street. (Courtesy of Thelma Tice.)

The shortage of building materials during World War II slowed housing construction, but development continued in College Park as new subdivisions soon pushed beyond the city limits. The Nydegger Investment Company platted Interlaken in 1941 on the former Nydegger farm on the northwestern edge of College Park. The Interlaken Addition, shown here, extended the development past Lake Sarah to Lake Fairview in 1946. (Courtesy of Carrie Busbee.)

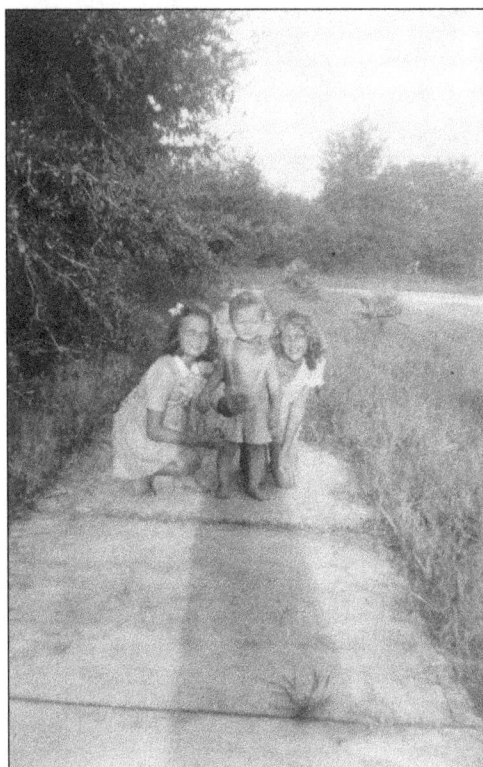

In this 1944 photograph, Grace and Bill Wendorff play with their neighbor Judy Huggins on the sidewalk near their grandparents' house at 610 Rugby Street. The end of the land boom left undeveloped areas of overgrown bushes and tall grass among the new houses, giving parts of College Park a rural appearance, evident here despite the proximity to the Edgewater Drive business center. (Courtesy of Grace Chewning.)

Erna Achenbach moved her College Park Kindergarten to her home on Steele Street in 1945 following the death of her husband, Fritz. When the successful kindergarten attracted more students than the house could accommodate, Erna held classes on the screened porch. Some classes met in the yard, and by 1949, her establishment became the Open Air School. (Courtesy of Irma Scudder.)

Before the public schools included kindergarten, Erna Achenbach offered preschool and kindergarten. Some children continued at the popular Open Air School through the first grade before enrolling at Princeton Elementary School. Many College Park photo albums include group images of children in their costumes from the annual plays and pageants presented at the school. (Courtesy of Irma Scudder.)

The children in this 1949 photograph taken at Erna Achenbach's Open Air School clearly did not want to be in the picture. The flower costumes and rabbit ears suggest that this group appeared in a spring program. Many College Park families still treasure photographs of their children from the popular plays, but, uncharacteristically, every child's face in this photograph registers disgust. (Courtesy of Irma Scudder.)

Children at Concord Park School dress as flowers and pixies for May Day in 1947. Tunnels built in 1950 under Colonial Drive and the Orange Blossom Trail provided safe passage to the school for College Park children. Soon after the tunnels opened, the state highway department widened and straightened Colonial Drive to become the busy State Road 50. Concord Park School closed in 1964. (Courtesy of Bertie Hunt.)

Third grade students at Concord Park School in 1948 pose for their class photograph on the school lawn. Their teacher, Rhea Anderson, stands at far right in the third row. Most of the girls wear Brownie uniforms, and several boys in Cub Scout uniforms stand behind them in the second row. College Park schools and churches sponsored Scout troops for boys and girls. (Courtesy of Bertie Hunt.)

Amos Reath ran a gas station at 1420 Edgewater Drive and Shady Lane Drive in the 1920s, and Fred Tegder followed in 1937. Robert Penland bought the property and business from Tegder in 1946. With his five sons (from left to right) Ralph, Lat, Ford, Albert, and Bobby, shown here around 1954, Robert Penland operated a grocery and gas station at that corner for more than a decade. (Courtesy of Lana Mathews.)

Richard Magee worked behind the pharmacy counter at Albert Drug Store in 1960. Arnold and Stanley Albert moved the drugstore from downtown Orlando to the corner of Princeton Street and Edgewater Drive in 1946. The old-fashioned store with its community message board and popular soda fountain became an institution in College Park. (Courtesy of Elizabeth Magee.)

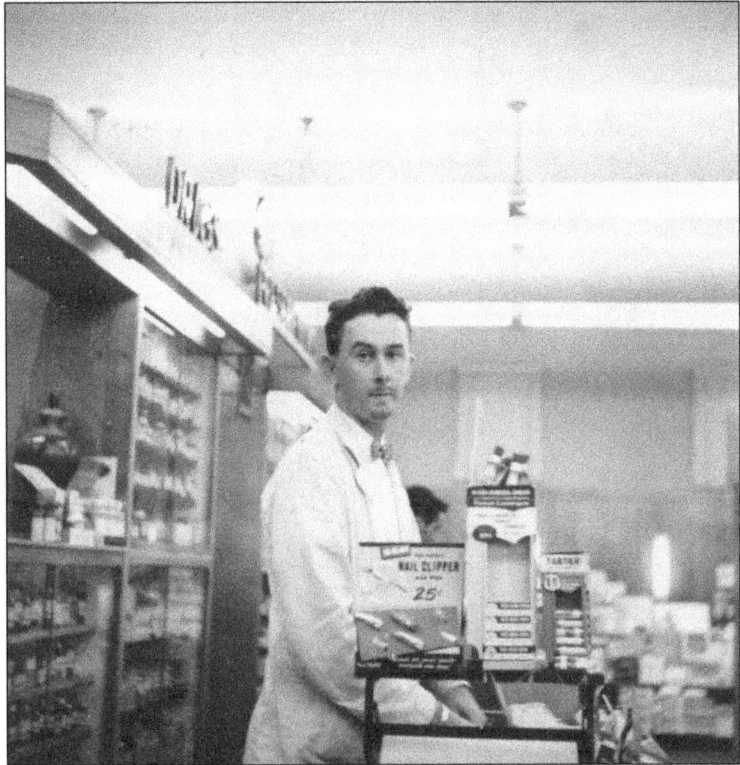

Albert Drug Store became a popular place to meet friends for sodas and hamburgers, as well as purchase pharmaceutical needs, cosmetics, and toiletries. A College Park institution, the store occupied the corner of Edgewater Drive and Princeton Street for 46 years, closing when Arnold Albert retired in 1992. (Courtesy of Elizabeth Magee.)

During the land boom of the 1920s, it seemed that everyone bought and sold real estate. The postwar housing crisis in the late 1940s and the 1950s again offered opportunities for builders and realtors. L.M. Lippitt, formerly a clerk with the Orange County government, opened a real estate office at the corner of Edgewater Drive and Harvard Street, shown here in 1948. (Courtesy of Debra Bremiller.)

In 1949, Ruby Wren Cole, shown cutting the cake, celebrated the 10th anniversary of Wren's Red & White grocery store at 2200 Edgewater Drive. Wren's and Harrison's grocery stores occupied the same block of Edgewater Drive for 10 years. Wren's continued in business through 1967, competing with one or more other grocery stores, including Publix after 1948. (Courtesy of Bunny Parish.)

Pictured here on Mother's Day 1955, the Rev. Howard Gress, pastor of Calvary Presbyterian Church, holds Luanne Murphy, the baby he baptized that morning. Other children he had baptized since his arrival as pastor in 1949 joined him in front of the church at 709 Edgewater Drive. Baby boom children filled Sunday Schools in churches of every denomination. (Courtesy of Luanne Preston.)

An enterprising photographer with a pony visited College Park in 1948, and the children showed the same delight at having their pictures taken as their parents had in the 1920s. Pictured here is Bertie Martin, dressed in cowgirl clothes at her home at 830 Ellwood Avenue. (Courtesy of Bertie Hunt.)

Bertie Martin taught her little brother Eddie to drive his kiddie car on Ellwood Avenue in 1949. The smooth brick street, curbs, and sidewalk indicate a well-planned neighborhood south of Lake Adair, though the large lawns and vacant space suggest a sparsely populated one. Children played in the street with no fear of the traffic interrupting their games. (Courtesy of Bertie Hunt.)

College Park developer J. Carl Tegder platted Lake Silver Shores early in 1949, and before the end of the year, Tegder had lined the streets of his new subdivision with houses under construction. D. Leon and Sophia Hope bought the first lot on the left in this 1949 photograph, and Tegder built their concrete block house at 913 Silver Drive. (Courtesy of Lynda Swenk.)

Lee Hope and his daughter Lynda visit the construction site of their new home in 1949. The sign in front of the house indicated financing backed by the Federal Housing Administration. Part of the New Deal National Housing Act of 1934, the FHA insured loans for home building and regulated interest rates and terms of mortgages, enabling more families to own homes. (Courtesy of Lynda Swenk.)

The West Smith Street gang gathered for this photograph in 1949. With the end of World War II, new houses for returning servicemen and their families filled every vacant lot and spilled over into new subdivisions. A phenomenon of the general optimism and security, the postwar baby boom populated many neighborhoods with gangs of playmates. (Courtesy of William Castlen.)

This photograph records Linda Flynn's enchantment with the pony a photographer brought to her back yard at 500 Harvard Street in 1949. College Park's many children undoubtedly kept the photographer busy; on some streets children lived in nearly every house, and the pony did not have far to walk between photographs. (Courtesy of Linda Flynn.)

College Park, with its small-town atmosphere and values, was always a good place for children. Here, in the backyard of his home at 838 Ellwood Avenue in 1949, Eddie Martin shows off the string of fish he caught in nearby Lake Adair, where fishing was safe and legal. (Courtesy of Bertie Hunt.)

The sidewalk in front of her home at 500 Harvard Street, near University Drive, gave Linda Flynn a great place to roller skate and to learn to ride her brand new tricycle in 1949. The palm trees and the Mediterranean-style house in the background, the sidewalk, and the abundant landscaping suggest that College Park had become an established community. (Courtesy of Linda Flynn.)

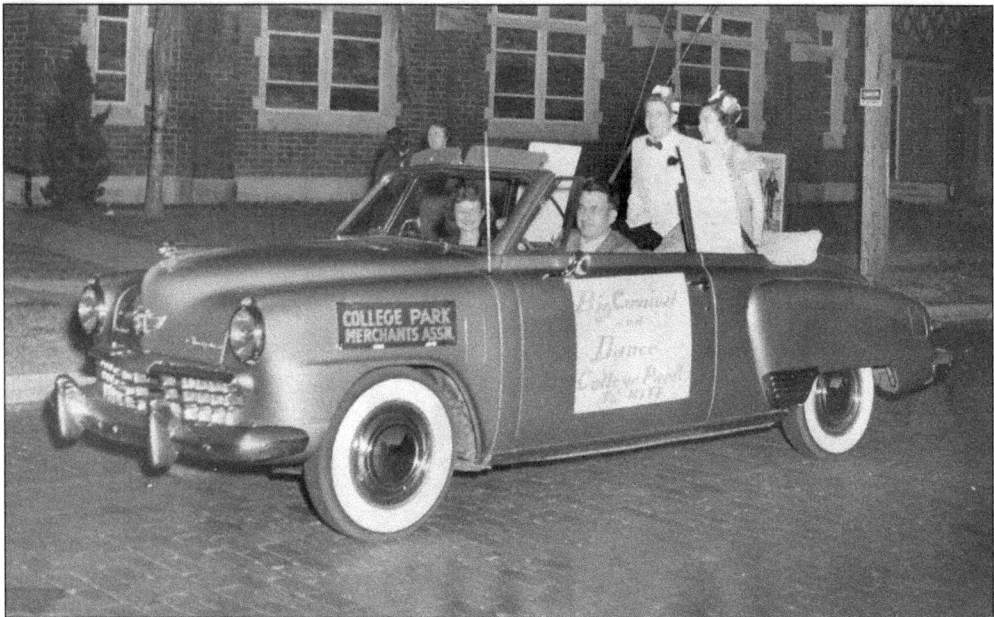

Jerry Chapman and Marylynn McEwen, king and queen of the 1949 College Park Christmas Fair, pass the College Park Methodist Church in a parade sponsored by the College Park Merchants Association. The sign on the convertible promises a "Big Carnival and Dance Tonite." The parade began at Lake Adair and continued on Edgewater Drive, which was paved with bricks. (Courtesy of Debra Booth.)

Lynda Hope remembers the day in 1950 when a photographer brought a pony to Silver Drive, and she has the photograph her parents bought showing her excitement at riding it. The photographer found the perfect neighborhood for his enterprise in College Park, with its many children and prosperous families. (Courtesy of Lynda Swenk.)

The children attending the College Park Baptist Church Vacation Bible School in 1946 gather in front of the 1928 church building. The steady increase in available housing in College Park that began with World War II continued into the postwar period, and new families with young children quickly filled the new houses. (Courtesy of College Park Baptist Church.)

The College Park Baptist Church completed its first unit, used as a sanctuary and Sunday school, in 1949. This photograph places it on Edgewater Drive with the original church built in 1928. The church later demolished the original building and replaced it with a new sanctuary in 1963. (Courtesy of College Park Baptist Church.)

The College Park Baptist congregation outgrew its church in the years during and after World War II. Membership increased from 189 in 1945 to more than 1,500 in 1959. New buildings in 1949 and 1954 provided educational space, and in 1963, the church issued $600,000 in bonds for a new sanctuary, shown here in 1963 during construction. (Courtesy of College Park Baptist Church.)

The rapid growth of College Park after the war convinced the Episcopal diocese of the need for an Episcopal church in College Park. St. Michael's Episcopal Church started in 1948 as a mission church meeting in Duckworth's Garage on Edgewater Drive, as pictured here. The congregation moved in 1949 to a small chapel in a former storefront on Edgewater Drive. (Courtesy of St. Michael's Episcopal Church.)

St. Michael's Episcopal congregation acquired property on North Westmoreland Drive in 1950 and built the first church building there in 1951. In 1958, they moved into a new sanctuary on the same property, and the original building, seen here in the 1950s, became the parish hall. The congregation later named it Quigley Hall in honor of Fr. Vernon Quigley, rector for 28 years. (Courtesy of St. Michael's Episcopal Church.)

Around 100 College Park women met in May 1949 to organize a woman's club to help manage a city recreation program. College Park at that time had no recreation place or community center. The women formed the College Park Woman's Civic Club, raised money, and broke ground for a community clubhouse near Dartmouth Park in February 1951. (Courtesy of Marilyn Ferris.)

The College Park Woman's Civic Club joined the Federation of Women's Civic Clubs late in 1950. The club hosted meetings and recreational events, and raised money through bazaars and block drives to build and maintain their clubhouse. Among other civic endeavors, in 1954, the Junior Women's Club assisted during the fire department's Clean Up week. (Courtesy of Marilyn Ferris.)

The ladies of the College Park Woman's Civic Club gather for President's Tea at their clubhouse in 1956. In 1959, the clubhouse remained the only center for recreational, youth, and civic activities in College Park, and the Woman's Civic Club hoped to enlarge and renovate the building. (Courtesy of Marilyn Ferris.)

One of the greatest female athletes, Mildred "Babe" Didrickson Zaharias, relaxes with her husband, wrestler George Zaharias, at Dubsdread Country Club in the 1950s. A frequent participant in amateur and professional golf tournaments at Dubsdread, Babe excelled at most sports. She began to play golf in 1935 and became a charter member of the Ladies Professional Golf Association in 1950. (Courtesy of Carl Dann III.)

The Dubsdread golf course hosted many tournaments over the years, attracting the best professional golfers. Here Babe Didrickson Zaharias and George Bolesta oppose Sam Sneed and Betty McKinnon in the Orlando Open International Mixed Two-Ball Tournament at Dubsdread in 1953. Sneed and McKinnon won that year. In the 1951 tournament, Zaharias and Bolesta defeated Patty Berg and Pete Cooper. (Courtesy of the Tap Room at Dubsdread.)

Professional dancer Edith Royal operated a dance school on Edgewater Drive from 1955 until 1985. Her husband's work brought her to Orlando in the 1940s, and she opened her first dance school in 1949. Bill Royal soon became her business manager, running three schools with more than 1,000 students by 1985. Her Ballet Royal performing corps began Orlando's tradition of *The Nutcracker* in 1964. (Courtesy of Carol Meyer Parker.)

Ruth Pounds taught ballroom dancing and etiquette in her home on Clifford Drive from about 1935 until the mid-1950s, when the classes became too large and the zoning board closed the school. Pounds found a location on Edgewater Drive and opened her first studio in 1955. Formal dances at the Country Club of Orlando concluded each year's classes. (Courtesy of Peggy Jo Van den Berg.)

College Park young people learned dancing and etiquette at Pounds Dance Studio. Along with the popular dances of the day, students learned the waltz, tango, and other classical ballroom dances. Lessons in etiquette prepared them for social situations requiring proper behavior. Pictured here are Pounds students gathered at the Country Club of Orlando for their formal dance around 1960. (Courtesy of Peggy Jo Van den Berg.)

American novelist and poet Jack Kerouac lived in this house at 1418 Clouser Avenue in College Park while he waited for publication of his best-known novel, *On the Road*, in 1957. A Beat Generation pioneer, Kerouac typed his trademark spontaneous prose without interruption on paper taped end-to-end in long scrolls. He wrote *The Dharma Bums* while living in the Clouser Avenue house. (Courtesy of Grace Hagedorn.)

Irma Achenbach Scudder leads her class at the Open Air School on a tour of the vegetable garden around 1950. The outdoor space at the Steele Street location included several playgrounds and study areas, as well as a garden where the children could learn how food grows. (Courtesy of Irma Scudder.)

The 1953–1954 kindergarten class at the Open Air School assembles on the playground jungle gym with their teacher for their class photograph. During its 50 years in College Park, the innovative kindergarten on Steele Street became a community institution. It started in 1931, when the public schools did not yet include kindergarten, and eventually offered classes for children from ages three to five and first through third grades. In the early years, Erna Achenbach went door-to-door in search of students to enroll. In later years, parents who had attended the school themselves sent their children to the Open Air School. The outdoor classes came about when the school's own success forced Erna to creatively deal with the lack of space in her small house. The Open Air School closed in 1981. (Courtesy of Irma Scudder.)

The children in Katherine Carlton's first grade at Princeton School in 1951 seem to have coordinated their poses for this photograph. All the girls except one near the center crossed their left legs over their right, and all the boys folded their arms. (Courtesy of Princeton School.)

The North Orlando Senior High School PTA took office in April 1952, before the death of William R. Boone prompted the school board to rename the South Orlando school for the longtime principal of the old Orlando High School, which closed at the end of the 1952 school year. South Orlando became Boone High School, and North Orlando became Edgewater High School. (Courtesy of Edgewater High School.)

Edgewater High School opened with two classroom buildings, shown here in 1952. The gymnasium, cafeteria, and auditorium completed the new campus, dedicated in September 1952 on a 20-acre tract on Edgewater Drive. The school board purchased the property in 1949, and broke ground in May for the new high school, which cost $905,040. (Courtesy of Edgewater High School.)

Edgewater High School opened for classes in September 1952, but in April, less than six months before school started, the campus still lacked landscaping. Jeanette Lott, PTA grounds chairman, led the beautification program to plant shrubs and flowers around the new buildings. (Courtesy of Edgewater High School.)

Orville R. Davis served as principal of Edgewater High School from its opening in 1952 until he retired 10 years later. The auditorium, one of the four original buildings, functioned as the activities center for the new school. In 1989, following a $1 million refurbishment, it became the Orville R. Davis Auditorium. (Courtesy of Edgewater High School.)

This aerial photograph taken soon after Edgewater High School opened shows the auditorium, two classroom buildings, and a building housing the gymnasium and cafeteria. An oval track and baseball diamond make up the school's sports complex. The vacant, grassy-looking property around the school and on the opposite side of Edgewater Drive suggests a somewhat remote location in 1954. (Courtesy of Edgewater High School.)

With the Depression and World War II in the past, Carl Tegder built a house for himself on five lakefront lots in his 1925 Palm Terrace subdivision. The house at 1133 Bryn Mawr Street, shown here in the mid-1950s with Lake Silver in the background, resembles the California ranch style, rather than the Mediterranean or Craftsman bungalows typical of College Park. (Courtesy of Julie Williams.)

The Rex-McGill Investment Company platted Lake Ivanhoe Heights in 1952, and it is likely it built this house at 2000 Ivanhoe Road at that time. Lowndes Lippitt, standing in the front yard in this 1955 photograph, bought the house in 1952. Its design seems more ranch-like than bungalow, a trend that became increasingly popular in 1950s housing construction. (Courtesy of Debra Bremiller.)

Built in the late 1940s, this house at 1124 West Smith Street seems to combine the traditional cottage style with the developing California ranch design. Wellborn Phillips bought the property in 1939, along with about 400 others, from Nonnarb Properties, which acquired it after the Cooper-Atha-Barr Company bankrupted itself trying to honor land boom mortgage commitments. Phillips built affordable houses for returning servicemen. (Courtesy of William Castlen.)

Mary Lippitt enjoys the yard, while Agnes Koehler waits on the porch in this 1955 photograph of the Koehlers' house at 2600 Harrison Avenue. Built around 1950 in the Anderson Park subdivision, the spacious lawn and ranch style appearance of the house suggest its later construction date and location in a newer part of College Park. (Courtesy of Debra Bremiller.)

College Park families overwhelmed Princeton Elementary School in the 1950s, when children born during the postwar baby boom reached school age. To relieve overcrowding at Princeton Elementary School, construction began in 1952 on a second elementary school north of Princeton on Lake Silver. When Lake Silver School opened in 1953, Princeton transferred 100 students to the new facility. (Courtesy of Lake Silver School.)

The Lake Silver Elementary School, under construction in this 1953 photograph, occupies the corner of Vassar Street and Rio Grande Avenue, just inside the Orlando city limits at that time. The Rugby Street water tower in the background stood in the first block west of Edgewater, with the second tower farther east on Hazel Street at Cornell Avenue. (Courtesy of Lake Silver School.)

The officers of the newly formed Lake Silver Elementary School PTA pose with the school principal, Morita Mason Clark, in 1953. Children living in the new subdivisions on the northern edge of College Park attended the more conveniently located Lake Silver School. Nearby Fairvilla School closed in 1955, two years after Lake Silver opened. (Courtesy of Lake Silver School.)

When Lake Silver Elementary School opened in 1953, students bought their lunches from the "Henry Chuck Wagon," a school bus converted to a food truck. Orange County lunchroom supervisor Elma Henry designed the bus to replace the cafeteria the school lacked funds to build. The students bought a hot lunch from the chuck wagon daily while they awaited the cafeteria. (Courtesy of Lake Silver School.)

Every day, the Henry Chuck Wagon stopped at Fairvilla School to pick up food for the Lake Silver Elementary School students' lunches. The converted school bus parked next to the lunchroom building, where the children enjoyed lunch served from the chuck wagon. The school board eventually built a modern cafeteria for Lake Silver School. (Courtesy of Lake Silver School.)

Lake Silver School's expansion with additional buildings and the all-important cafeteria began in 1953, soon after the school opened. Preparing the construction site, Principal Morita Clark rode on the front of the tractor, while an unidentified man drove and two passengers joined him on the back. (Courtesy of Lake Silver School.)

Students from Lake Silver School enjoy roller-skating at the Coliseum in the mid-1950s. The large Moorish building on North Orange Avenue near Lake Ivanhoe opened on December 23, 1926, and for nearly 50 years, the Coliseum, its swimming pool, and bowling alley provided space for dances, shows, and other recreation. (Courtesy of Lake Silver School.)

From left to right, Lake Silver Safety Patrol boys Robert Barden, Roger Sanders, Richard Houghton, John Kehoe, and William Castlen wait in Orlando for the train to take them to Washington, DC, in 1956. Each year the school principal selected boys to represent Lake Silver School in the annual rally and National School Patrol Parade down Pennsylvania Avenue. (Courtesy of William Castlen.)

The Princeton School Patrol Boys, and one Patrol Girl, visit Orlando mayor William Beardall in his office in 1951. The students acted as crossing guards on busy streets near Orlando schools, lending official assistance to the city police department. Princeton became a four-lane street not long after the Safety Patrol program began helping children to cross. (Courtesy of Princeton School.)

In 1954, eight reindeer brought Santa Claus and his sleigh to the Princeton Elementary School Christmas program. According to school policy, every child had a part in the programs presented at the school. College Park grew dramatically in the late 1940s and into the 1950s. By 1952, the school added three portable buildings to accommodate the increased student population. (Courtesy of Princeton School.)

Bess Coe's kindergarten class gathered for this photograph in the mid-1950s. Bess opened a kindergarten at her home at 1308 West Princeton Street in 1948, just in time to enroll the first children of the baby boom generation. The public schools did not offer kindergarten or preschool at that time, and most College Park parents sent their children to a private kindergarten. (Courtesy of Bunny Parish.)

Robert E. Lee Junior High School majorettes (from left to right) Pat Christman, Jenelle Hawthorne, Beverly Arnold, Linda Flynn, and Vickie Hagy stand at attention in 1960. By the 1950s, as College Park expanded farther north, Memorial Junior High in downtown Orlando no longer met the needs of the growing population. Lee Junior High opened in September 1955 on Maury Road between Lake Fairview and Lake Silver. (Courtesy of Linda Flynn.)

Orlando's changing demographics following World War II brought an increase in the Catholic population, prompting the Catholic Diocese of St. Augustine to purchase land in 1952 for a new parish and a central Catholic high school north of College Park. Work began in 1954 on the St. Charles Borromeo Parish School, the first wing of which is shown here in 1955. (Courtesy of Archives of the *Florida Catholic*.)

The St. Charles Borromeo Parish, established on March 31, 1954, built a parish school and a high school before starting its church building. Edgewater High School offered St. Charles Borromeo the use of its auditorium for Sunday mass until the parish completed the Bishop Moore High School building, seen here in 1957 through the arch at St. Charles School. (Courtesy of Archives of the *Florida Catholic*.)

Fr. Vincent Smith checks the progress of foundation construction for the Bishop Moore High School girls' school building in 1959. Boys and girls studied in separate classes at Orlando's only Catholic high school, opened in 1955 on the grounds of St. Charles Borromeo Catholic Church in College Park. (Courtesy of Archives of the *Florida Catholic*.)

The Diocese of St. Augustine held its 1959 Eucharistic Congress at St. Charles Borromeo in College Park. A platform built over Little Lake Fairview accommodated the altar and the clergy, with chairs set under the trees on the grounds of the new parish for the several thousand worshippers expected to attend. (Courtesy of Archives of the *Florida Catholic*.)

The College Park Grandmothers Club held its board meeting in September 1955 at 2000 Ivanhoe Road, the home of Mary Lippitt. Their names have been lost, but the ladies, their children, and their grandchildren probably all lived within a few blocks of one another. Families settled in College Park to stay, sometimes for several generations. (Courtesy of Debra Bremiller.)

Marvin Coram, who lived on Western Way, and Ben McGuffey, of Bryn Mawr Street, show off the fish they caught in Lake Silver around 1950. The clear and pristine lake in its rural setting offered good fishing for many families who lived in the nearby subdivisions. (Courtesy of the Kelsey Family.)

The Barnes family poses for a photograph at 2812 North Westmoreland Avenue in 1957. From left to right are (first row) Peggy, Bill, Bob, and Joan; (second row) Dora Barnes, Elizabeth Barnes, Lincoln Barnes, and Abraham Lincoln Barnes. Lincoln Barnes established Barnes Draperies on North Orange Avenue in 1952. (Courtesy of Robert Barnes.)

Bob and Bill Barnes admire the advertising on their father's car in 1961. Abraham Lincoln Barnes Jr. retired from Dickson and Ives Department Store in Orlando on a Friday in 1952 and opened Barnes Drapery and Floor Coverings at 2008 North Orange Avenue the following Monday. The brothers assumed the management of the business when their father passed away in 1991. (Courtesy of Robert Barnes.)

Ethel Flynn and her daughters Karen and Linda pause in front of Dick Heim's camera shop in 1951. In 1948, when Dick Heim built his camera shop at 1825 Edgewater Drive, it shared the block with Oscar Murphy's filling station. After a decade of business growth in the 1950s, ten other establishments had joined Heim's shop on that block of Edgewater Drive. Heim's closed in 1970. (Courtesy of Linda Flynn.)

College Park children crowd a float in the Christmas parade on Edgewater Drive in 1953. Santa Claus appeared on another float sponsored by the College Park Downtown Merchants Association. Much of College Park's business growth came in the 1950s, when vacant lots along Edgewater Drive filled with commercial buildings and stores selling necessities from hardware to toys and pharmaceuticals to groceries. (Courtesy of Bunny Parish.)

The masonry crew, pictured here in 1954, gathers at the Kelsey Construction office at 306 East Princeton. The company started in 1920 and built houses in College Park, as well as larger buildings, including the McCall Office Building at 1209 Edgewater Drive, the College Park Baptist Church's first unit, and the new College Park Publix. (Courtesy of Kelsey Construction Inc.)

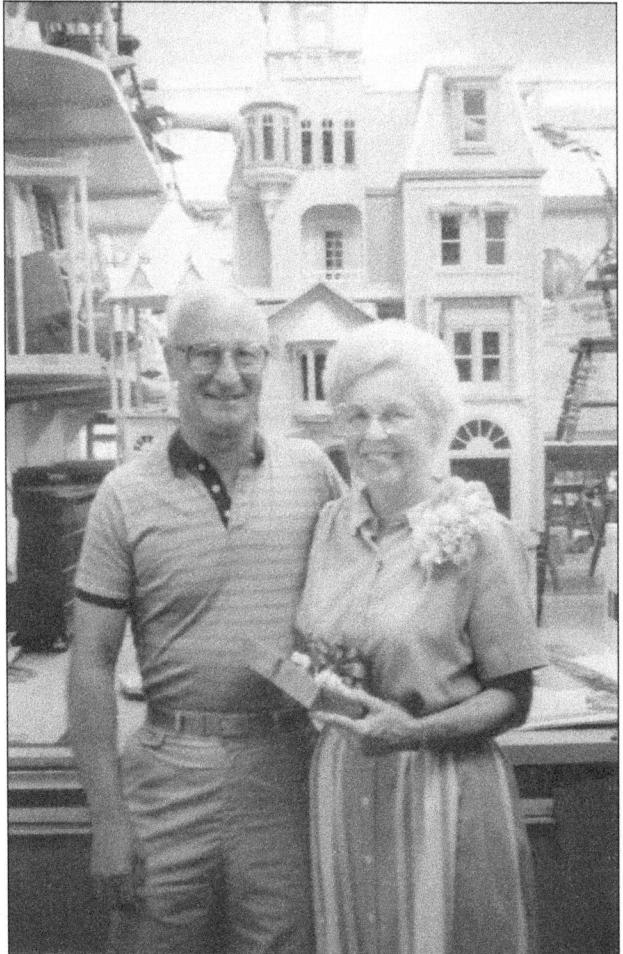

Robert L. and Betty Bruner, shown here on their retirement in 1988, opened the Toy Parade on Edgewater Drive in 1957 because they needed a gift for their daughter's birthday. They sold the store 31 years later. Known for its elaborate dollhouses and personal service, the independent toy store closed in 1994 when it could no longer compete with large national chains. (Courtesy of Diane Patrick.)

This Craftsman bungalow at 710 West Harvard Street, photographed around 1930, came down in the 1950s to clear the site for a new College Park Publix market. Publix operated a grocery store at the corner of Harvard Street and Edgewater Drive for more than 60 years. (Courtesy of Phoebe Carpenter.)

As commerce expanded in College Park, business owners moved to establish a community bank. The College Park National Bank of Orlando, an affiliate of the First National Bank of Orlando, opened in October 1952 on Edgewater Drive at Vassar Street. The bank bought more property at the same location for a larger building in 1955, and in 1982 it became Sun Bank of College Park. (Author's collection.)

By the late 1950s, Edgewater Drive businesses provided for most of College Park residents' needs, from food and clothing to sporting goods and Christmas toys. With the growth, College Park also acquired traffic. Looking south past Voorhee's Gulf station, College Park Cleaners, and Albert Drugs, the College Park Methodist Church appears in the background on the left, followed by the Publix supermarket. (Courtesy of Debbie Goetz.)

Duckworth's Garage stood on the northwest corner of Edgewater Drive and Yale Street in 1956, beside Butler's Atlantic service station. A little farther down, Yazoo Lawn Mower Center and Hall's Barbershop flanked Pickerill's Sporting Goods. Rose DeLuxe cleaners occupied the opposite corner, with the Publix down the street. The numerous garages and gas stations underscored the growing importance of automobiles. (Courtesy of State Archives of Florida, Florida Memory.)

At the corner of Edgewater Drive and Smith Street in 1956, Walton's Rexall Drugs faced Voorhee's Gulf station. Businesses north of the drugstore included Gerry's Dress Shoppe, Gerry's Children's Wear, Sammie Bethea's restaurant, and Wilson's shoe store. Beyond the gas station, on the east side of Edgewater, the large white building housed the new College Park National Bank of Orlando. (Courtesy of State Archives of Florida, Florida Memory.)

By 1957, businesses lined Edgewater Drive north of Princeton Street. Wren's Red & White anchored one end of the block that included Fenton's Radio and Appliance, McCall's photography, and Johns Hardware. Albert Drugs led off on the opposite side of Edgewater, followed by College Park Florist, Palm Terrace beauty salon, Kirstein printers, The Cake Box bakery, College Park dry cleaner, and Stewart Jewelry. (Courtesy of State Archives of Florida, Florida Memory.)

Four

COMMUNITY BUILDING

The end of the 1950s marked the end of College Park's most dramatic period of growth. Homes or building sites replaced most of the vacant land. Stores, offices, and gas stations lined Edgewater Drive. The baby boom children moved through the schools, but with the end in sight, the existing schools added rooms and portable units, but no new schools opened in College Park after the 1950s.

The 1960s began with a hurricane, a rare experience for an inland city, but even more destructive than the hurricane, Interstate 4 sliced through the east side of College Park taking out homes and businesses along its right-of-way. Many College Park residents protested what they saw as the destruction of Lake Ivanhoe, divided with a causeway and a bridge to carry the new road across the lake. All but six of the streets running east to west between Edgewater Drive and North Orange Avenue closed, disrupting daily life and dividing the community. The new highway opened in 1966 with a dedication on the Lake Ivanhoe bridge.

College Park rallied against a school board attempt to close Princeton Elementary School in the early 1970s, compiling population studies and persuasive arguments that kept the neighborhood school open. The business community organized in the 1980s to fight a restrictive commercial zoning change, and the College Park Neighborhood Association formed to protest a traffic issue. In the face of threats to the neighborhood, whether from a hurricane, a highway, or government, College Park fought back as a community. Out of the struggles, a stronger, more united College Park emerged.

Hurricane Donna came from the southeast on September 10, 1960, with 105-mile-per-hour winds. The high winds brought trees down on houses, vehicles, businesses, and power lines, and four inches of rain caused flooding and widespread damage in College Park. This photograph, taken on September 11 in northwest College Park, shows some of the damage. (Courtesy of Jane Roney.)

College Park acquired another banking institution in 1961 with the opening of the College Park branch of the First Federal Savings and Loan in a new $225,000 building on Edgewater Drive. The name changed several times after Great Western Financial Corporation acquired the bank in 1991. (Courtesy of Jerry Porter.)

The George Stuart family, pictured at top from left to right, Georgia Lee, Georgia "Vicki," Jacob, George Jr. (standing), Charlie, George Sr., and Robert F., welcome the newest member of the family, Geneva Ann, to the family Christmas card in 1960. The cards became a College Park tradition beginning with the birth of the Stuarts' first child in 1946. All of the children graduated from Princeton Elementary School and Edgewater High School, and the Stuarts established a family tradition of public service in business, political, and civic affairs. George Sr. served in the city government, Charles in the family office supply business, Jacob with the chamber of commerce, and George Stuart Jr. as city commissioner and from 1978 to 1989 as a Florida state senator. Robert represents College Park as a city commissioner. (Courtesy of Orlando city commissioner Robert F. Stuart.)

The original St. Charles Borromeo Catholic Church, dedicated in 1958, appears in the middle of this 1960 photograph, with the St. Charles School to its left and Bishop Moore High School on the right. Edgewater Drive, at lower right, remained a two-lane road in 1960. (Courtesy of Archives of the *Florida Catholic*.)

Orlando's Catholic population grew in the postwar years, particularly after the Martin Company, now Lockheed-Martin, moved its operations from Baltimore to Orange County in 1957. Many employees bought houses in College Park and in the nearby Pine Hills development. In 1968, when the Diocese of St. Augustine divided to create the new Diocese of Orlando, St. Charles Borromeo became its cathedral. (Courtesy of Archives of the *Florida Catholic*.)

On October 1, 1976, fire swept through the St. Charles Cathedral, destroying the building's interior and its contents. Parishioners who had helped build the church 20 years earlier watched in shock. The diocese relocated the cathedral to St. James Parish in Orlando, and the St. Charles Borromeo congregation rebuilt their church. A charred crucifix remains from the old cathedral. (Courtesy of Archives of the *Florida Catholic*.)

St. Charles Borromeo Parish built a new church after the fire destroyed the interior of the church building in October 1976. The exterior walls of the old building remained standing, allowing the structure to be salvaged for offices, meeting rooms, and a preschool. On November 4, 1979, the parish dedicated the new church, built in a distinctive, modern style. (Courtesy of Archives of the *Florida Catholic*.)

Vietnamese Catholics who came to Orlando in 1975 following the fall of Saigon shared temporary space in many churches, including St. Charles Borromeo beginning in 1987. After 20 years of St. Charles's hospitality, Thanh Philipphe Phan Van Minh Catholic Church moved to its own building on Par Street in 2007. (Courtesy of Archives of the *Florida Catholic*.)

Edgewater High School entered its second decade with additional buildings and more playing fields, though the football field still lacked stadium seating, relying instead on bleachers. This 1960s aerial photograph also shows significant development of the neighborhood around the campus. Commercial buildings seem to occupy every property on the opposite side of Edgewater Drive, vacant when the school opened in 1952. (Courtesy of Edgewater High School.)

Erna Achenbach, photographed with her daughter, Irma Scudder, in 1971, started her College Park Kindergarten in 1931, drawing on her training in Germany to create a unique school that served College Park families for 50 years. In 1949, it became the Open Air School. Irma Scudder taught kindergarten classes and became principal when her mother retired; the school closed in 1981 when Irma retired. (Courtesy of Irma Scudder.)

A new Fire Station Three, more centrally located on Elizabeth Avenue in College Park, replaced the old Station Three in 1973. This photograph from 1978 shows the old fire station cut in half to be loaded on flatbed trailers for the move to Loch Haven Park, a few blocks away. Restored and refurbished, it again houses fire trucks as a fire museum. (Courtesy of Dick Camnitz.)

The Anglican Church of the Incarnation, a parish in the Anglican Catholic Church, started as a mission in 1979. After several years in temporary quarters, the church built its first permanent home at 1523 Edgewater Drive in 1982. In 2012, the congregation became Incarnation Catholic Church. (Courtesy of Incarnation Catholic Church.)

The Incarnation Church congregation acquired the site of the ABC Liquor Store and Lounge at the corner of Edgewater Drive and Shady Lane Drive in 1990. After demolishing the ABC building, the church broke ground in September for the parish hall that would provide space for a nursery and Sunday school classes. (Courtesy of Incarnation Catholic Church.)

The College Park Merchants and Professional Association sponsored an annual sidewalk art festival beginning in 1969. An early College Park Art Festival is shown here on Edgewater Drive at Rugby Street. Held every year until 1982, when construction work on Interstate 4 and traffic congestion forced its cancellation, the two-day festival attracted thousands of spectators as hundreds of artists competed for cash prizes. Attempts to revive the College Park Art Festival failed, but other community events took its place. The Downtown College Park Partners sponsor annual events on Edgewater Drive, including Holiday on the Drive (an evening opportunity for early Christmas shopping), Jazz on the Drive, and Dancing on the Drive. The College Park Neighborhood Association sponsors Sunday in the Park, an annual family community celebration at Dartmouth Park, an Easter egg hunt at Albert Park, and Movies in the Park. After nearly 100 years, community spirit and family-friendliness make College Park's 32804 a sought-after postal code. (Courtesy of Debbie Goetz.)

Visit us at
arcadiapublishing.com

••••••••••••••••••••••••••••••••••••••

www.ingramcontent.com/pod-product-compliance
Lightning Source LLC
Chambersburg PA
CBHW080614110426
42813CB00006B/1502